BOOKS IN THE ABICS PUBLICATIONS SERIES

Badiru, Deji, **8 by 3 Paradigm of Time Management: Balancing Work, Home, and Leisure**, iUniverse, Bloomington, Indiana, USA, 2013

Badiru, Deji, **Badiru's Equation of Success: Intelligence, Common Sense, and Self-discipline**, iUniverse, Bloomington, Indiana, USA, 2013

Badiru, Iswat and Deji Badiru, **Isi Cookbook: Collection of Easy Nigerian Recipes**, iUniverse, Bloomington, Indiana, USA, 2013

Badiru, Deji and Iswat Badiru, **Physics in the Nigerian Kitchen: The Science, the Art, and the Recipes**, iUniverse, Bloomington, Indiana, USA, 2013.

Badiru, Deji, **Physics of Soccer: Using Math and Science to Improve Your Game**, iUniverse, Bloomington, Indiana, USA, 2010.

Badiru, Deji, **Getting things done through project management**, iUniverse, Bloomington, Indiana, USA, 2009.

ABICS Publications
A Division of
AB International Consulting Services (ABICS)

www.ABICSPublications.com

Books for home, work, and leisure

8 by 3 Paradigm for Time Management

Balancing Work, Home, and Leisure

| Time for Work | Time for Home | Time for Leisure |

DEJI BADIRU

iUniverse, Inc.
Bloomington

8 BY 3 PARADIGM FOR TIME MANAGEMENT
BALANCING WORK, HOME, AND LEISURE

iUniverse books may be ordered through booksellers or by contacting:

iUniverse
1663 Liberty Drive
Bloomington, IN 47403
www.iuniverse.com
1-800-Authors (1-800-288-4677)

ISBN: 978-1-4759-8477-4 (sc)
ISBN: 978-1-4759-8478-1 (e)

Library of Congress Control Number: 2013907348

Printed in the United States of America.

iUniverse rev. date: 4/26/2013

DEDICATION

To the memory of late Omolade Bisola
Badiru, the flower who never had a time to
bloom; and shall remain a bud forever

TABLE OF CONTENTS

ACKNOWLEDGMENTS

I thank my family, friends, and professional colleagues, who constantly challenge me to find ways to be more time efficient and performance conscious in all that I do.

PREFACE

Are you constantly pressed for time? Do you always wish you had more time to do all that you have to do? Are you always pressed to meet deadlines? Are you facing challenges in balancing your work life and your home life? Do you often find yourself rushing to complete your assignments? Are multiple priorities keeping you disoriented? Do you face the futility of getting organized? Like most of the population, if you answer "yes" to any of these questions, the 8 by 3 Paradigm of Time Management is for you. The trick to getting things done on time is to find a formula for balancing both competing and complementing priorities. The pursuit of personal goals requires efficient time management. This is exactly what the 8 by 3 paradigm offers.

In the present day of a rushed economy and a crowded lifestyle, everyone needs a helping hand in balancing the work life and the home life. The challenges are often so great that we don't even have time to get the necessary help. In other words, we don't have time to learn time management techniques. So, any tool or technique of time management must be made simple and mnemonic enough to make it easy to remember and easy to apply. It is with this backdrop that I offer the 8 by 3 paradigm of time management based on my own direct practice of the technique for over 35 years. The "8 by 3 Paradigm of Time Management: Balancing Work, Home, and Leisure" explains the technique and illustrates how to apply it.

The overarching theme of The 8 by 3 paradigm of time management is to view time as the basis for everything we do. An efficient use of time is the foundation for success in all endeavors. Balancing time implies using explicit and equitable allotments of time to the various undertakings of each day. The development of the paradigm is based on my own personal practice of the approach for over three decades that have resulted in my ability to manage multiple endeavors as evidenced by my credentials summarized on the next page. The approach has been honed enough to the point that it can be shared with others who may want to adopt and adapt it for their own activities. The paradigm presents a simple guide to managing the hours of the day over three major blocks of time allocated to the three typical categories of human undertakings. The three blocks of time cover work activities, home activities, and leisure activities. Each block has sub-blocks that are managed in contiguous hierarchical timeline templates. With a target audience of working adults, the 8 by 3 paradigm can be customized for each person's specific needs and circumstances. The paradigm does not ask readers to sacrifice one time block for another or vice versa. Rather, it encourages balancing time across the work time, the home time, and leisure time because all three are essential for a complete and fulfilling life.

In addition to describing the 8 by 3 paradigm, this book also covers the constant passage of time, work breakdown structure, time breakdown structure, cost breakdown structure, measures of time efficiency, overcoming time robbers through activity time scheduling, work rate consideration, 5s principle for getting organized, and tips for 8 by 3 time management. Useful time-related conversion factors are presented in the Appendix at the end of the book.

Deji Badiru
April 10, 2013

AUTHOR'S CREDENTIALS FOR THE 8 BY 3 PARADIGM

In as much as the contents of the 8 by 3 paradigm of time management is based on the author's own direct experience and application of his unique approach to time management, it is essential to provide a summary of his credentials and qualifications for writing "8 by 3 Paradigm of Time Management: Balancing Work, Home, and Leisure."

Adedeji Badiru (pen name Deji Badiru) is Professor and Head of Systems Engineering and Management at the Air Force Institute of Technology. He was previously professor and department head of Industrial & Information Engineering at the University of Tennessee in Knoxville. Prior to that, he was professor of industrial engineering and Dean of University College at the University of Oklahoma. He is a registered professional engineer (PE), a certified Project Management Professional (PMP), a Fellow of the Institute of Industrial Engineers, and a Fellow of the Nigerian Academy of Engineering. He holds BS in Industrial Engineering, MS in Mathematics, and MS in Industrial Engineering from Tennessee Technological University, and Ph.D. in Industrial Engineering from the University of Central Florida. His areas of interest include mathematical modeling, project modeling and analysis, economic analysis, systems engineering, efficiency improvement, and productivity analysis. He is the author of 22 technical books and six non-technical guide books. Many of his books are on the topic of project planning and execution. He has also written 70 technical journal articles. He has 110 conference papers and presentations. He also has 25 magazine articles, 20 editorials and 12 newspaper commentaries. He is a member of several professional associations and several scholastic honor societies.

Deji Badiru has won several awards for his teaching, research, and professional accomplishments. He is the recipient of the 2009 Dayton Affiliate Society Council Award for Outstanding Scientists and Engineers in the Education category with a commendation from the 128th Senate of Ohio. He also won 2010 IIE/Joint Publishers Book-of-the-Year Award for co-editing The Handbook of Military Industrial Engineering. He also won 2010 ASEE John Imhoff Award for his global contributions to Industrial Engineering Education, the 2011 Federal Employee of the Year Award in the Managerial Category from the International Public Management Association, Wright Patterson Air Force Base, the 2012 Distinguished Engineering Alum Award from the University of Central Florida, and the 2012 Medallion Award from the Institute of Industrial Engineers for his global contributions in the advancement of the profession. In February 2013, he led a team that won the Air Force's Air University's 2013 award for Cost Conscious Culture (C3) for saving his unit over $300,000 in 2012 operational costs.

Deji Badiru has served as a consultant to several organizations and nations around the world including Russia, Mexico, Taiwan, Nigeria, and Ghana. He has conducted customized training workshops for numerous organizations including Sony, AT&T, Seagate Technology, U.S. Air Force, Oklahoma Gas & Electric, Oklahoma Asphalt Pavement Association, Hitachi, Nigeria National Petroleum Corporation, and ExxonMobil. He holds a leadership certificate from the University Tennessee Leadership Institute. He has served as a Technical Project Reviewer, curriculum reviewer, and proposal reviewer for several organizations including The Third-World Network of Scientific Organizations, Italy, National Science Foundation, National Research Council, and the American Council on Education. He is on the editorial and review boards of several technical journals and book publishers. Deji Badiru has also served as an Industrial Development Consultant to the United Nations Development Program (UNDP). He is also an accreditation Program Evaluator for ABET. In 2011, he led a research team to develop analytical models for Systems Engineering Research Efficiency (SEER) for the Air Force acquisitions integration office at the Pentagon. Deji Badiru has diverse areas of avocation. His professional accomplishments are coupled with his passion for writing about everyday events and interpersonal issues, especially those dealing with social responsibility. Outside of the academic realm, he writes self-help books, motivational poems, editorials, and newspaper commentaries; as well as engaging in paintings and crafts that can be viewed at www.badiru.com. He also manages a STEM-and-soccer education website for kids: www.physicsofsoccer.com. Deji Badiru is the founder of the Association of Military Industrial Engineers (AMIE): www.amienet.org. He has published books with John Wiley & Sons, Prentice-Hall, Chapman & Hall of England, Taylor and Francis/CRC Press, as well as other publishers. He started ABICS Publications (www.ABICSPublications.com) as an avenue to publish short non-technical guide books. Deji Badiru credits his own personal and professional accomplishments to the efficacy of the 8 by 3 paradigm of time management.

CHAPTER 1

THE 8 BY 3 PARADIGM OF TIME MANAGEMENT

"Divide and conquer your multiple priorities."
– Adedeji Badiru, Author

It is often said that one should not judge a book by its cover. That axiom holds true in most cases, but the "8 by 3 Paradigm of Time Management" is one book that can, directly, be judged by its cover. The design of the front cover tells the whole story of the 8 by 3 paradigm. The lessons of time efficiency conveyed in this book are embodied pictorially in the layout of the front cover design, which I developed specifically to succinctly represent the essence of the paradigm. The eight-hour blocks of time are gradient-color-coded sequentially, starting with the reference point of 0:00 hour and ending with the 24th hour of the day. Notice that the red zone represents the typical iniquitous hours of the day, when most of the naughty and bad things happen. This area leads into the yellow zone, representing the vibrant beginning of a new day. The green zone is next. This represents, roughly, the range of daytime hours when most of our productive activities occur. Notice the wide expanse of the green zone. The green zone fades into the gray zone, which represents the trailing off of the day. In the contiguous 24-hour representation, the gradient color coding starts from the blue zone and ends in the gray zone. The color-coding scheme and time block segmentation facilitate a better handle on how and where we allocate our precious hours each and every day. A disproportionate allocation of our very limited time is often the foundation for failure in personal projects. The clock-inscribed logo of the 8 by 3 paradigm is also embedded in the Front Cover.

BALANCING WORK AND HOME TIMES

The block-based time management approach of the 8 by 3 paradigm facilitates balancing of work life and home life. Recognizing where the time boundaries exist can help in allocating appropriate activities to each 8-by-3 block. In other words, give each block its due, time-wise. Working all the time or excessively outside the work-time block compromises the time allocation for home life. Conversely, staying at home all the time does not create a wholesome life. The 8 by 3 paradigm focuses on hierarchical allotment of time to three major blocks of human activities during a 24-hour day. As with any imprecise management scenario, there are no strict demarcation lines between the three 8-hour blocks of time. There is a continuity of time segments throughout the day. This sense of continuous involvement is often the source of poor management of time in common practice by most people. In the 8 by 3 paradigm, the idea is to adopt a conceptual segmentation of the day into three distinct, but contiguous 8-hour blocks of time, each with its own level of output accountability. Fuzzy overlapping of the blocks is allowed. The three 8-by-3 blocks of time are listed below and illustrated in the figure that follows:

1. Time for regular work
2. Time for home-based activities, including sleep
3. Time for leisure, rest, and relaxation activities

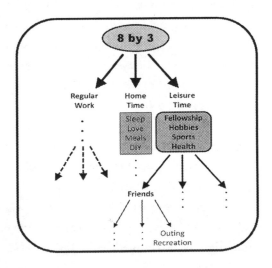

Motivational questions for each block of time include the following:

- What have I accomplished during this 8-by-3 block of time, in accordance with the expectations of the block?
- Have I slept enough, as expected during the 8-by-3 block of time?
- Have I contributed enough to the day's 8-by-3 block of work hours, as I was expected to do?
- Have I earned my salary for the day, as I should during the 8-by-3 block?
- Have I spent enough quality time with my family during their allotted 8-by-3 block of time?
- Have I taken sufficient break time for leisure, refresh, or recuperation during the 8-by-3 block?

Because of the contiguity of the blocks, a person may cannibalize time from the adjoining blocks on as-needed basis, as long as that does not become a permanent practice. You cannot compromise home-based family time for too long without suffering an adverse consequence. Similarly, you cannot cannibalize regular work time for long without running the risk of losing your job. Based on each person's personal desires, family situation, and social hierarchy of needs, the level of overlap will vary. However, always keeping the segmented blocks in mind helps to recognize professional commitments, family expectations, and social requirements. If you are an early riser, go to bed in time because it may be the only way to get enough sleep. Early risers tend to rise early no matter how late they go to bed. So, going to bed late may mean there will be no compensatory sleep time to make up the sleep deficiency. The generations-old adage below is still a very good inspirational guide:

"Early to bed and early to rise makes a man healthy, wealthy, and wise."
– Benjamin Franklin (1706 - 1790)

There are various combinations and permutations of activities. A potential list of desired, preferred, and imposed activities includes the following:

- **Regular salaried work**
- Regular business-hour work
- Extra work
- Overtime work
- Moonlighting work

- **Home-based activities**
- Family time
- Family meals
- Togetherness
- Companionship
- Kitchen projects
- Cooking chores
- Dining in and Dining out
- Sleep
- Laundry
- Child care
- Worship & Fellowship

- **Leisure activities**
- Exercise, Fitness, and Health
- Social connections
- Love and Friendship
- Vacation
- Hobbies and Sports

Notice that sleep is an explicitly scheduled requirement in the 8-by-3 paradigm. If sleep is not treated as a schedulable item, it becomes easily compromised and sacrificed in the usual race against time with respect to the competing demands on our time. Sleep should be treated as a high-priority requirement, whose allotment of time must be preserved. Occasional incursion into the sleep block of time is okay, as long as it does not become a habitual practice. Excessive borrowing from sleep time is akin to deficit spending. It will eventually catch up with the offender in terms of degradation of health. Personal wellbeing affects how well we use our time. So, we must invest in healthy pursuits. A healthy person is a more time-efficient person. There is always more to do than there is time to do. But, yes, you can do it all, if you are healthy, prudent, and disciplined. The time you invest in your health upfront will save you time and cost in healthcare services later on.

In understanding and preserving the time blocks in the 8 by 3 paradigm, it is essential to consider the importance of the following aspects:

Importance of work life:
- Income generation
- Professional connectivity
- Social pride
- Self-esteem
- Education

Importance of family time:
- Family bonding
- Wellness
- Support
- Moral support
- Mentoring
- Spiritual togetherness

Importance of sleep:
- Physical refresh
- Mental recuperation
- Health preservation
- Healing

A complementing pictorial representation of the 8 by 3 paradigm is presented below. My interest in time-blocking of activities started as long ago as 1974 when I was working as an accounts clerk in the Staff Pay Office of the Central Bank of Nigeria in Lagos, Nigeria. The nature of the job was that each accounts clerk was given a set of staff pay records to work on each day. The days leading up to a pay period were always a crunch time. I was someone whom the entire office recognized as always on time and keeping up with assignments with little or no accounting errors. Without realizing it at that time, I was actually practicing time blocking of the various activities that I was involved in each day, albeit not with the finesse described in the present 8 by 3 paradigm. Being an early riser, I would get to the office very early in the morning, well before the office opened. The first thing I did each day was to organize and reorganize my work desk. I would organize pencils, papers, and other office supplies in a specific way for each day. Once work started, I was efficient and effective in how I went about each day's tasks so much so that I would finish my workload for the day by lunch time. Even I was amazed and surprised at how quickly I was finishing ahead of everyone else. Once I finished, I would assist other colleagues for a couple of hours or so. Then I would set out juvenilely from the office to visit friends in other offices or go out to enjoy the sights and sounds of Tinubu Square, the iconic center of Lagos, where the Central Bank was located. If not that I had a good work record, the absence from my desk could be a matter requiring an official reprimand or a disciplinary action. But my office manager always looked the other way, electing to give me the freedom and flexibility to engage in other activities once my official assignment for the day was done. There was one particular colleague (name withheld) who would always make incriminating jokes about my absence from my desk. My manager always ignored him. The manager would, instead, remind everyone to be "as conscientious as Mr. Badiru has been with his assignments." Based on this, I started documenting my office organizational skills in the form of notes to myself, not realizing that the notes would be useful in later years for writing my project management books. I left the Central Bank of Nigeria in December 1975 to proceed to the USA on a full government scholarship to study Industrial Engineering, which I was later to find out has the official professional definition of being "concerned with the design, installation, and improvement of integrated systems of people, materials, information, equipment, and energy by drawing upon specialized knowledge and skills in the mathematical, physical, and social sciences, together with the principles and methods of engineering analysis and design to specify, predict, and evaluate the results to be obtained from such systems." This definition fits my time management practices perfectly. I have since always strived to "think like an industrial engineer and act like an industrial engineer." Even today, I still go about my work with the same youthful exuberance of my

Central Bank work time management practices. Getting things done on time is always a source of happiness for me. You, too, can create a platform of happiness for yourself by using the 8 by 3 paradigm to balance work, home, and leisure times.

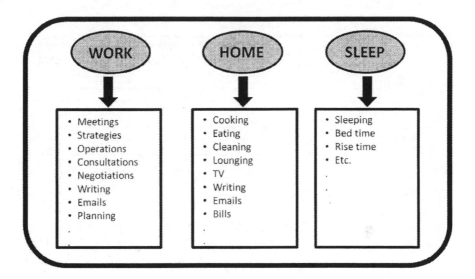

AVOIDING CRUNCH TIME

Being able to respect and sustain each 8-by-3 time block means being efficient and effective with the activities in each block. You can avoid crunch-time problems by following the suggestions below:

- Give each task its own allocation of one of the 8-by-3 blocks of time.
- Embrace every task within its own block of time. That is, a block for every task and a task for every block.
- Don't let unnecessary or low-value activities occupy your time.
- Do not do during one block of time what is best done in another block of time.
- Reserve daytime hours for what needs to be done during daylight.

The table below gives some examples of block-based scheduling of activities. You can expand and play around with your own items added to the list, as you wish. For those engaged in education rather than a paid employment, the education requirement should be handled as a deliberate work engagement with all the rights and dedication of the 8 by 3 time allocation. For those combining work and school, the 8 by 3 paradigm is still applicable and effective for balancing work, school, and home times.

Activities	Morning Block	Mid-Day Block	Evening Block	Night Block
Writing checks to pay bills			X	
Doing taxes			X	
Family time	X		X	
Salaried work		X		
Online shopping			X	X
Mowing the lawn	X	X		
Writing a book (unless it is fulltime job)			X	X

THE ESSENCE OF THE WORK LIFE

Time management within the work life is essential for the overall wellbeing of a person. If work time is managed effectively, there will be a reduced need for work to encroach upon the home life. The major time robbers at work are frivolous pursuits, chitty-chatty (chit-chat) engagements, and proliferation of back-and-forth emails. Opening, reading, and replying to emails consume much of the time of workers. In the early days of office emails (mid 1980s), supervisors worked hard to encourage workers to use emails. As an engineering faculty member at the University of Oklahoma in the 1980s, I remember the Dean of Engineering, Dr. Billy Crynes, actively pressing faculty to embrace communication via emails. Around 1987, he would randomly send email broadcasts to all engineering faculty around 6 a.m. on selected days. The first three faculty members to respond to him would get to have a free lunch with him. In the initial days of the ploy, there were very few takers. I recall that I was usually one of the three lucky first responders. As more faculty members got more at ease with email tools, protocols, and processes, there was an explosive jostling by faculty members to be the first to respond. Dean Crynes quickly became overwhelmed with offering free lunches. Having accomplished his goal of introducing faculty to email usage, Dean Crynes abandoned the program only after three months. Faculty email usage was never the same thereafter, as faculty members freely embarked upon self-directed proliferation of emails. Nowadays, workers wish they had fewer emails to attend to. Many express their chagrin of ever engaging in emails. But there is no going back. Email usage has become a part and parcel of the evolution of human communication, not only in the office environment, but also in home and community engagements. Since we cannot avoid it, we should find ways to manage it, with respect to time efficiency. Some time-focused tips for managing emails are presented below:

- Remember that to reduce receiving emails, you need to reduce your own sending of emails. Each email you write invites one or more emails that you have to deal with, thereby consuming more of your precious time.
- Don't send an email unless you really need to.
- Delete emails promptly if they don't need to be saved. Saved emails require more time to manage, review, sort, and deal with later on.
- Avoid Reply-All, if not needed. Replying to all creates opportunities for "All" to send you new emails, thereby requiring you to spend more time responding.
- Keep emails brief. Longer emails proliferate, mushroom, and re-germinate to consume more of your time.
- Use brief subject-line-only emails, if possible, to get your point across. Think of a twitter-type communication. This approach is great for "Thank you" notes.
- Use EOM (End of Message) on subject lines to indicate no need to open the email body if the subject line adequately conveys the essence of the communication, thus saving email handling time.

THE ESSENCE OF THE HOME LIFE

The home life is the essence of our life. Managing the home life effectively leads to happiness, satisfaction, and contentment. The home life is a reflection of what makes us who we are. At home, we engage in a wider variety of activities than in a typical work environment. The diversity of the home life can range from a single household, a married household, a childless household, a single-kid household, a household of multiple kids, a roommate household, and relatives household to a community-residents household. Each one requires different approaches to managing the relevant tasks, goals, and objectives. Even the physical structure of the house can impact how time is managed in the household. For example, single-family houses, condos, and apartment complexes may imply different approaches to managing time based on influences and interactions with other individuals. In a single household, just as in a multiple-person household, comparative benchmarks of how others handle certain chores may affect how you manage your own chores. I have always argued that siblings within the same age range growing up in the same household create developmental benchmarks and examples for themselves. Managing time in home-life chores may benefit from the following tips 8 by 3 paradigm tips:

- Allocate sufficient time for family interactions.
- Identify desirable family-time activities, such as eating together, group outing, sports, watching favorite TV programs, watching movies, visiting, and vacation travel.
- Use the kitchen as a frequent congregation point for the family. So, keep it organized, comfortable, and accessible.
- Establish family traditions early. Later-year establishments are more difficult and require more time.
- Communicate family values to everyone. It saves time by avoiding corrective pursuits later on.
- Establish an assignment of home chores and tasks upfront. This helps manage task execution time later on.
- Allocate family time at the earliest opportunity because time invested earlier on saves time in later family pursuits.
- Make a commitment to execute assigned chores promptly.
- Dedicate time to each item that has to be done. Letting an item drift consumes more time in the attempt to find a slot for it.
- Avoid serendipitous scheduling of unannounced family engagements.
- Keep the family block to be the family block, recognizing that occasional cannibalizing of time from one 8 by 3 block to another may become necessary, but it should be done within reason.

One good way to multitask tasks across the 8 by 3 blocks is to involve the family in appropriate tasks outside the home segment as much as possible and practical. This is particularly effective for the work life and home life time blocks. This may include family outing, joint involvement in sports events, spectator activities, shopping, work-related receptions, conference attendance, business-and-pleasure travels, remodeling, spring cleaning, and writing projects. I personally practice this approach frequently in my own use of the 8 by 3 paradigm. My spouse accompanies me to almost every open work-related social gathering. We attend many conferences, picnics, parties, and receptions together, thereby ensuring that some of my home-life togetherness requirements are satisfied while I am meeting work-related requirements. My professional colleagues know her more and she also knows a lot of my professional associates through our joint conference attendance. This saves me time whenever I need to explain to my wife about what and what happened to which colleague x, y, or z. Along the same line, when I was the newsletter editor for the Oklahoma City Chapter of the Institute of Industrial Engineers in the early 1990s, I would ask the print shop not to fold our newsletters. I would, instead, bring home printed newsletters so that my entire family could participate in the folding chores. It used to be a fun family event. My wife, Iswat, my two kids at that time, Abi and Ade, and I would share out the 200 newsletter copies at 50 copies per person. This way, no one person got over-burdened while we had fun together. We would even have competitions on who could finish his or her share of folding assignment first. Not only did this approach fulfill a family togetherness opportunity, it also allowed the family to become familiar and more supportive of my professional activities. Almost every book that I have written has one aspect of contribution or another from my family members in terms of proofreading, drawing a graphic, suggesting an idea, or typing. As an example, the sub-title for my book on the "Physics of Soccer: Using Math and Science to Improve Your Game" was suggested by my son, Ade. Ade and Abi were taught to type at an early age so that they could participate in my book manuscript typing chores. Although they are both grown now and have charted their own successful professional paths, they still remain a part of my professional activities through consultations, interactions, and frequent exchanges of documents and ideas. This approach saves me time when seeking their inputs on crucial professional decisions. The joint cookbook with my wife on "Physics in the Nigerian Kitchen: the

Science, the Art, and the Recipes" is another avenue of a family project that fulfills a dual purpose of a professional pursuit coupled with a household interest. As with many close family projects, a discord of opinion can develop. If that happens, a fun and amicable resolution can be devised. My family had split opinions on how the cookbook should be titled. To settle the split, we wrote a second joint cookbook with a different twist entitled "Isi Cookbook: A Collection of Easy Nigerian Recipes." It was a fun, rewarding, and time-saving undertaking.

THE ESSENCE OF SLEEP TIME

It is generally believed that we spend between 25% and 35% of our life sleeping. This is based on a total overall life assessment. The times, obviously, vary on a day-by-day basis, depending on what is going on in each day. The recommended amount of sleep per day is eight hours, which is 33.33% of the day. Although rarely do we accomplish this on a day-by-day basis, it is important to recognize and preserve that block of the day. This is one of the main premises of the 8 by 3 paradigm of time management. If this block of time is consistently compromised, it can lead to adverse effects on health and wellbeing. This detrimental impact may be so gradual that the individual hardly notices it. When health issues do develop later on, it is difficult to trace them back to the long-term effect of sacrificing sleep. Each person's genetic makeup does influence reactions to sleep patterns. But, by and large, over a long stretch of time, having a sufficient sleep is crucial for each person. Occasional needs may necessitate waking up too early or sleeping extremely late. If these are balanced out by occasional compensatory sleep, things should even out over time. If you are a morning person, use the morning hours for the most tasking activities. Don't wake up early just for the sake of waking up early. Do something worthwhile in the early waking hours. Below are some tips for ensuring adequate sleep under the 8 by 3 paradigm of time management:

- Make sleep a priority, just as you would any other high-priority requirement.
- End work when work needs to be ended.
- Establish a specific time to go to bed, with plus or minus allowances, as may be needed.

- Go to bed early if you are an early riser, it may be the only way to ensure you sleep long enough.
- Put everything else aside and focus on a restful sleep when it is your time to sleep.
- Don't attempt to perform a function requiring a high level of cognition and concentration when you are sleepy. For example, sleeping while driving leads to many fatal accidents annually. The National Sleep Foundation (www.sleepfoundation.org) reported in 2009 that 1.9 million drivers have fatigue-related car crashes or near misses each year in the USA. No doubt, each accident causes those involved an enormous loss of time, if not loss of life. Sleep deprivation causes loss of time in terms of the effectiveness of performing tasks.

THE ESSENCE OF LEISURE TIME

Leisure time provides us an opportunity to recuperate and rejuvenate the body, soul, and mind. Balancing leisure time with the other essentials makes for a complete, rewarding, and gratifying existence. We should not overindulge in leisure or any of the other essentials. Leisure time should be distinguished from time for business, work, or household chores, although a careful choreographing can overlap leisure with the other essentials. The 8 by 3 paradigm facilitates an explicit allocation of time spent away from work and home-based domestic chores, even if overlapping becomes unavoidable. My own leisure activities include reading, writing, cooking, painting, dancing, watching favorite TV programs, and sports fan-ship. Reading printed newspapers is one of my highly-coveted daily leisure activities. Cooking, as listed here, does not represent an undertaking as a domestic chore, but rather as an object of relaxation and culinary experimentations, which are gratifying for me. It also creates an opportunity for being a kitchen member of the household, which is another aspect of family togetherness. In the days that I played soccer or coached my kids' soccer teams, we used the entire family attendance at games as a group leisure activity. This is another example of satisfying a leisure requirement and family togetherness with the same event that we all enjoyed. Don't consider leisure time as idle time or wasted time because it is fulfilling its intended purpose. The quote below makes this point aptly:

> "Time you enjoy wasting is not wasted time."
> – Marthe Troly-Curtin

WORK ETHICS AND ETHICAL STANDARDS

Following the requirements of the 8 by 3 paradigm has the desirable side effects of upholding good work ethics and abiding by ethical standards. With respect to good work ethics, personal morality and work responsibility should be inculcated into time management practices. Taking accountability for what needs to be done rather than taking evasive or defensive paths will result in good outcomes both in the short term as well as the long term. Whining is a time robber. Constructive whining may be necessary in some cases to bring a problem to the attention of leadership, with an offer of a solution option. Destructive whining simply complains and wastes time without offering a solution to the prevailing problem. With respect to ethical standards, the code of ethics of a relevant profession can help uphold and advance the integrity, honor, and dignity of the person. The engineering and medical fields, along with others, offer rigorous code of ethics that individuals may draw upon. Work ethics and ethical standards directly influence physical wellbeing, mental alertness, teamwork, sportsmanship, wingman-ship, selflessness, and leadership in ways that lead to efficient time utilization later on.

THE BENEFITS AND EFFICACY OF THE 8 BY 3 PARADIGM

To recap, the 8 by 3 paradigm conveys the concept of balancing time over the three general categories of home, work, and leisure. While a strict adherence to time blocking may not be possible always, it is expected that the paradigm will serve as a continual reminder of the importance of balancing time requirements. The benefits to be obtained from using the 8 by 3 paradigm include the following:

- Balancing time allocations for work, home, and leisure activities
- Balancing competing and complementing priorities
- Reducing search time for items in the home or office
- Reducing time for household chores
- Getting organized for more efficient chores at home or office
- Straightening out personal goals with respect to time allocations
- Recognizing the constant passage of time
- Becoming proficient with time-cost tradeoffs
- Allocating time efficiently across multiple objectives
- Taking drudgery out of household chores
- Conserving energy in the pursuit of tasks
- Getting family together for fun and fellowship projects
- Minimizing labor-intensive run around when executing tasks

CHAPTER 2

THE CONSTANT PASSAGE OF TIME

"You may delay, but time will not."
– Benjamin Franklin

Efficient management of time matters a lot, from the standpoint of personal and professional development. This chapter summarizes this view in the axiom aptly stated below:

It is not how much time you have that is important, but how well you use the time that you have.

We talk much about saving money and accumulating wealth. But we don't commit as much emotion and energy to saving time and accumulating accomplishments. Time is money. Therefore, time deserves an equal treatment according to the 8 by 3 paradigm of time management. Every minute counts, just as every dollar matters in our personal pursuits. Time waits for no one. My own poem, echoed in the diagram below, emphasizes the constant passage of time in accordance with the Benjamin Franklin quote at the beginning of this chapter.

The Flight of Time

What is the speed and direction of Time?
Time flies; but it has no wings.
Time goes fast; but it has no speed.
Where has time gone? But it has no destination.
Time goes here and there; but it has no direction.
Time has no embodiment.
It neither flies, walks, nor goes anywhere.
Yet, the passage of time is constant.

© Adedeji Badiru, 2006

A lot of fluff exists in our day-to-day activities. Oftentimes, those who claim not to have enough time to do what needs to be done are those who mismanage their time. If fluff can be removed from our activities, more time will be available to accomplish meaningful pursuits. It is important to get busy and stay busy. Time is used more efficiently when there is more to do. Idle time is frittered away unproductively. When fully loaded with tasks, we are forced to manage our time more carefully. Otherwise, we will be tempted to postpone and defer activities, with the end result that not as much is accomplished time wise. For example, it is my own personal and direct observation, as an educator, that students not taking a full load of classes in college tend to perform poorly academically because time is squandered by putting studying off again and again.

The theme throughout the 8 by 3 Paradigm of Time Management is to identify and highlight the time implications in everything we do. If time is managed tactically, we can succeed with almost everything. Time is precious in the sense that it is through time that we accomplish our goals and objectives. Time is irrecoverable in the sense that time, once lost, cannot be regained. Time is incompressible in the sense that the passage of time itself is fixed, even though the time-based duration of a task may be condensed or elongated. Time is relative, in the sense that different people use time differently with different contexts.

Getting things done on a daily basis is a matter of efficient allocation of time and resources. Time, as a limited commodity, must be utilized efficiently. Resources, as a scarce asset, must be managed effectively. I am often asked by my colleagues and my students about how I manage to get many things done, seemingly effortlessly. My usual answer cites the use of time-based activity management, focusing on high-value activities and eliminating unimportant activities. Urgent items are treated as urgent and executed promptly to get them out of the way. This requires forsaking procrastination every time a temptation to put things off develops. Important items are scheduled and done at the earliest convenient time opening. The figure below presents some guidance for evaluating the relative importance and urgency of activities. I use this approach for my multiple activities in book manuscripts, personal pursuits, family activities, professional associations, and work-related administrative duties.

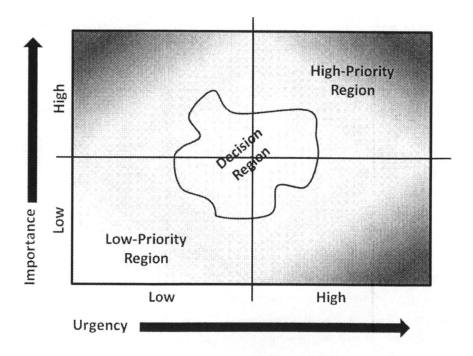

It is my belief that there is a time factor in everything we do. Even a simple activity such as conserving water has eventual time implications. For example, the more gallons of water you use, the higher your water bill will be. The higher your water bill is, the more work you have to do to earn enough money to pay the higher water bill. The more money you have to earn, the more time you will need to work to earn the money. So, time utilization is the end result. Consequently, conserving water, in addition to its environmental benefits, does have time saving implications for the individual person. This is an extreme example, but it typifies the premise of the 8 by 3 paradigm of time management. The same rationale can be applied to other human challenges, such as preventive maintenance of a vehicle, cooking in batches rather than in spurts, and using clean-as-you-go housekeeping practices. If you love to cook for gatherings, you don't have to cook for every gathering. You may occasionally use precooked items from a grocery store. Many wholesale food outlets and membership clubs, such as Sam's Club, offer a variety of pre-packaged options. You may cook for every other gathering or so, such that the audience can still appreciate your cooking prowess and special recipes. Large-scale cooking for every gathering every time consumes a lot of time and may detract you from other high-value time-sensitive goals. The key is to reduce the number of time-consuming chores that may lead to a rushed pursuit of other high-value engagements. Haste makes waste and can result in reworks that are time costly.

One accomplishment a day puts 365 accomplishments within reach in one year. This is plenty of room to do what you need to do. So, don't whine about time; get going with your time-based pursuits. Time efficiency enhances your chances for professional success and it emphasizes your commitment to excellence.

HASTE MAKES WASTE

More time is wasted doing things over than doing them correctly in the first place. More time taken up front to do something well the first time saves a lot more time later on. Errors happen when we allow haste to creep into our activities. Such errors then require time to correct, thereby encroaching on the time allotted for the next activity. The correction time constitutes a waste and should be minimized. Always give yourself some wiggle room. Getting yourself in a tight corner will cost you more time.

PREEMPTION IS BETTER THAN CORRECTION

My own common approach to implementing the 8 by 3 paradigm is my philosophy that "preemption is better than correction. Preempting problems can avoid the need for disruptive corrective actions later on. A key aspect of managing the time blocks is to strictly control what goes in each block in the first place. By preempting potential problems, we can conserve precious time to allow us to perform each task within its reasonable block of time. The common saying below emphasizes this point:

> "If you don't have time to do it right the first time,
> when would you have time to do it over?"

PROCRASTINATION IS PROBLEMATIC

Procrastination is an abomination in the 8 by 3 paradigm. Unnecessary procrastination is nothing more than chucking accountability and responsibility. There is never a better time to perform a task than at its first opportunity. Procrastination does not give you more time; it simply gets things cramped up later on. Activities should be done when they come up to be done. Each missed opportunity leads to deficit scheduling of pending activities. Very much like deficit spending, procrastination puts a person in the situation of having to play catch up. Do what you must when you first have the time to do it. You may not have a subsequent opportunity to do it. The quotes below cogently convey this point:

> "Only put off until tomorrow what you are
> willing to die having left undone"
> – Pablo Picasso

> "You cannot escape the responsibility of tomorrow by evading it today."
> – Abraham Lincoln

THE VALUE OF A MINUTE

What is your minute worth? When people ask you to do something that only takes a couple of minutes, be sure to consider how much your "couple of minutes" is worth. Serendipitously committing a minute here and a couple of minutes there will result in a lot of your time going down the drain and intractable. Another important aspect of time assessment is to recognize how much an engagement actually costs you. A one-hour meeting often will cost you a lot more than one hour, considering the additional time requirements to disengage from what you were doing before the engagement and the extra time needed to get back to speed after the engagement ends. I refer to these additional boundary times as "set-down" time and "re-ramp-up" time. Using this principle, it can be seen that a one-hour engagement can consume a lot more time because of the pre and post time requirements. Many people don't account for these extra times and they end up wondering why not much gets done in an average work day. When I invite many people to a meeting or a gathering, I am always conscious of the collective time of the group. So, I endeavor to use the collective time efficiently and effectively. The sum of minutes from the work times of several high-salaried employees can amount to a significant productivity loss and dollars unaccounted for. I end this chapter with an extract from an article that I wrote in 1996 on the value of collective time at meetings.

DEJI BADIRU'S PERSPECTIVES ON MEETINGS

Parkinson's Law says, "Work expands to fill the available time."

Deji Badiru's mutation of the law says, "Talk expands to fill the available time."

Meetings represent one avenue for information flow and knowledge sharing for group decision-making. Effective management of meetings is an important skill for any administrator or manager. Unfortunately, meetings often degenerate to time-wasters; consequently obstructing productivity and detracting from other essential functions. This is because most meetings are poorly organized, improperly managed, called at the wrong time, or even unnecessary. In some organizations, meetings are conducted as a matter of routine requirement rather than necessity. While meetings are essential for communication and decision-making, they accomplish nothing if not managed properly. A meeting of 30 people wasting only 30 minutes, in effect, wastes 15 full hours of work time. That much time, in any organization, amounts to thousands of dollars in loss of productive work. It does not make sense to use a one-hour meeting to discuss a task that will take only five minutes to perform. This is analogous to hiring someone at an annual salary of $100,000 to manage an annual budget of $5,000. In 1993, a newspaper columnist and humorist, Dan L. Stewart, wrote about management meetings:

"Management meetings are rapidly becoming this country's biggest growth industry. As nearly as I can determine, the working day of a typical middle manager consists of seven hours of meetings, plus lunch. Half a dozen years ago at my newspaper, we hired a new middle management editor with an impressive reputation. Unfortunately, I haven't met her yet. On her first day at work, she went into a meeting and has never come out."

Stewart concludes his satire with "I'm expected to attend the next meeting. I'm not sure when it's scheduled exactly. I think they're having a meeting this afternoon about that." In the past, when an employee had a request, he went to his boss, who would say "yes" or "no" right away. The whole process might take less than one minute out of the employee's work day. Nowadays, several hierarchies of meetings may be needed to review the request. Thus, we may have a departmental meeting, a middle management staff meeting, upper management meeting, executive meeting, steering committee meeting, ad hoc committee meeting, an off-site retreat, and a meeting with outside consultants, all for the purpose of reviewing the simple request. My perspectives about meetings are summarized below:

1.   Don't call for a meeting, unless it is absolutely needed.
2.   Most of the information passed out at meetings can be more

effectively disseminated through simple memos. Emails should be fully exploited to replace most meetings.

3. The point of diminishing returns for any meeting is determined by the number of people that are actually needed for the meeting. The larger the number of people at a meeting, the lower the meeting's productivity. The extra attendees only serve to generate unconstructive and conflicting ideas that only impede progress.

4. Not being invited to a meeting should be viewed as an indication of the high value placed on an individual's time within the organization.

5. Regularly scheduled meetings with specific time slots often become a forum for social assemblies; if not managed properly.

6. The satirical adjourn time of a meeting is equal to the scheduled start time plus five times the number of agenda items minus the actual start time. The subtraction of the start time is to encourage calling the meeting to order promptly. The longer the start time, the less time is available for the actual business. If the start time is immediate, then total meeting time is allocated for conducting actual business. If the actual start time coincides with the scheduled end of the meeting, then there will be no time left to hold the meeting. Because it is difficult to do away with all meetings, we must maximize the output of the meetings that do take place by using the guidelines below:

1. Do pre-meeting homework.
   a. List topics to be discussed (agenda).
   b. Establish the desired outcome for each topic.
   c. Determine how the outcome will be verified.
   d. Determine who really needs to attend the meeting.
   e. Evaluate the suitability of meeting time and venue.
   f. Categorize meeting topics (e.g., announcements, important, urgent).
   g. Assign time duration to each topic.
   h. Verify that the meeting is really needed.
   i. Consider alternatives to the meeting (e.g., memo, telephone, electronic mail).

1. Circulate written agenda prior to the meeting.
2. Start meeting on time.
3. Review agenda at the beginning.
4. Get everyone involved; if necessary employ direct questions and eye contacts.
5. Keep to the agenda; do not add new items unless absolutely essential.
6. Be a facilitator for meeting discussions.
7. Quickly terminate conflicts that develop from routine discussions.
8. Re-direct irrelevant discussions back to the topic of the meeting.
9. Retain leadership and control of the meeting.
10. Recap the accomplishments of each topic before going to the next. Let those who have made commitments (e.g., promise to look into certain issues) know what is expected of them.
11. Have empathy for those invited to meetings and end meeting on time

Regardless of the structure and expediency exercised in conducting meetings, the real work is done behind the scene. Note that, as social animals, we sometimes need separate "social meetings" where we can have all the chips and drinks we want and take all the time that we want to discuss irrelevant topics. One of my favorite definitions of a meeting is "the confusion of one man multiplied by the number of people present."

CHAPTER 3

WORK BREAKDOWN STRUCTURE

"The nucleus of a task is in splitting it in two"
– Adedeji Badiru, Author

Work is best accomplished in smaller chunks of efforts that are organized hierarchically. The technique of Work Breakdown Structure (WBS) is commonly used for this purpose. It is a simple approach to representing the foundation over which a goal is developed and managed. WBS refers to the itemization of a project for planning, scheduling, and control purposes. WBS defines the end goal or scope of a project. The WBS diagram presents the inherent components of a project in a structured block diagram or interrelationship flow chart. WBS shows the relative hierarchies of parts (phases, segments, milestone, etc.) of the endeavor. The purpose of constructing a WBS is to analyze the elemental components of the project in detail. If a project is properly designed through the application of WBS at the project planning stage, it becomes easier to estimate time requirements for the components of the project. Project control is also enhanced by the ability to identify how the components link together. Tasks that are contained in the WBS collectively describe the overall project goal. A large project may be broken down into smaller sub-projects that may, in turn, be systematically broken down into task groups. As conveyed in the opening quote for this chapter, the essence of a task is found when the task is divided into its components. WBS permits the implementation of a "divide and conquer" concept for project control. This fits the purpose of the 8 by 3 paradigm introduced in this book.

Individual components in a WBS are referred to as WBS elements, and the hierarchy of each is designated by a Level identifier. Elements at the same level of subdivision are said to be of the same WBS level. Descending levels provide increasingly detailed definition of project tasks. The complexity of a project and the degree of control desired will determine the number of levels in the WBS. Each component is successively broken down into smaller details at lower levels. The process may continue until specific project activities (WBS elements) are reached. In effect, the structure of the WBS looks very much like an organizational chart. The 8 by 3 paradigm mimics a WBS-type breakdown of a 24-hour day.

A simple and familiar example of the application of the WBS structure is the purchase of a new car. In this case, "Car Purchase" is the final goal. Some of the lower-level objectives include "Get Finance," "Sell Old Car," "Trade-in Old Car," "Clean Old Car to get it ready for the market," "Consult with insurance agent," and "Do market research of latest car models." These can be organized into hierarchical levels to form a structure of how the eventual goal can be accomplished. The basic approach for preparing a WBS is as follows:

Level 1 WBS: This level contains only the final goal. For the purpose of implementing the 8 by 3 paradigm, this item should be identifiable directly as a personal need with respect to the prevailing environmental factors, such as home, work, family, and leisure.

Level 2 WBS: This level contains the major sub-sections of the goal. These sub-sections are usually identified by their contiguous locations or by their related purposes.

Level 3 WBS: This level of the WBS contains definable components of the level 2 sub-sections. In operational terms, this may be referred to as the finite details level of the end goal.

Subsequent levels of WBS may be constructed in more specific details depending on the span of control and flexibility desired. If a complete WBS becomes too crowded, separate WBS layouts may be drawn for the Level 2 components. In order to make a WBS for the 8 by 3 paradigm practical for an individual, the goals and objectives should consider the scope of effort, resource requirements, and feasibility of the endeavor. Sometimes, we tend to be over-ambitious with our undertakings with respect to time availability, time requirement, resource requirement, resource availability, and our own capability to deliver. Such a misjudgment of personal capability often spells doom and failure in getting things done.

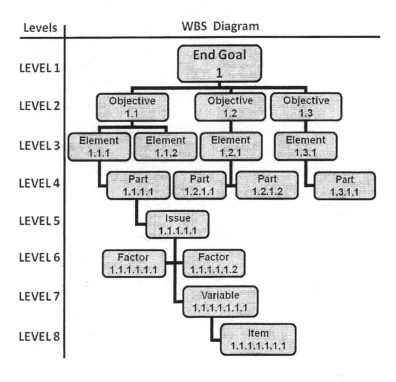

The 8 by 3 paradigm is very amenable to personal customization for the user's specific situation and prevailing needs. Each person must determine where and how each block of time can be allocated. The key requirement is to have the self-discipline, fortitude, and personal dedication to stick with the time allotments. A popular Nigerian Yoruba saying provides the following guidance:

"You cannot use someone else's clock to set your own work schedule."

You must map your own capability and personal references to the requirements of the job, with the eventual goal of getting the job done well and on time.

CHAPTER 4

TIME BREAKDOWN STRUCTURE

"If it weren't for the last minute, nothing would get done."
– Rita Mae Brown

As humans, we love living on the edge of time. The opening quote above highlights the importance of last-minute execution of our task responsibilities. As illustrated in the hour-glass diagram below, the passage of time ticks and must be allocated efficiently from one stage of work to the next stage. In the same way that a work breakdown structure is developed, a time breakdown structure can also be developed for implementing the 8 by 3 paradigm of time management. Time management is the process of identifying specific actions to be performed to produce the deliverables of a project. The basic requirements are the following:

- Create a WBS structure that identifies time-based deliverables at the lowest level (e.g., work packages and due dates).
- Decomposed work packages into smaller timed activities (e.g., work duration start and end points).
- Use the smaller activities for estimating, scheduling, executing, monitoring, and controlling the flow of work and 8 by 3 time allocations.

The concept of SMART (Specific, Measurable, Aligned, Realistic, and Timed) is useful in accomplishing a time breakdown structure of projects as listed below:

Specific: Tasks in the breakdown structure must be specific.
Measurable: Tasks in the breakdown structure must be measurable.
Aligned: Tasks in the breakdown structure must be aligned and achievable within the overall project goal.
Realistic: Tasks in the breakdown structure must be realistic and relevant to the organization.
Timed: Tasks in the breakdown structure must have a time basis.

Crashing is the expediting or compression of activity duration. Crashing is done as a trade-off between a shorter task duration and a higher task cost. It must be determined whether the total cost savings realized from reducing the project duration is enough to justify the higher costs associated with reducing individual task durations. If there is a delay penalty associated with a project, it may be possible to reduce the total project cost even though crashing increases individual task costs. If the cost savings on the delay penalty is higher than the incremental cost of reducing the project duration, then crashing is justified. Normal task duration refers to the time required to perform a task under normal circumstances. Crash task duration refers to the reduced time required to perform a task when additional resources are allocated to it.

If each activity is assigned a range of time and cost estimates, then several combinations of time and cost values will be associated with the overall project. Iterative procedures are used to determine the best time or cost combination for a project. Time-cost trade-off analysis may be conducted, for example, to determine the marginal cost of reducing the duration of the project by one time unit. Critical chain is the theory of constraints applied to project management specifically for managing and scheduling projects and controlling critical path activities. Constraint management is based on the principle that the performance of a system's constraint will determine the performance of the entire system. If a project's characteristic constraint is effectively managed, the overall project will be effectively managed. This is analogous to the belief that the worst performer of an organization will dictate the performance of the organization. Similarly, the weakest link in a chain determines the strength of the chain. Because overall operation is essentially a series of linkages of activities, one break in the linkage determines a break of the overall operation. That is, it takes only one negative to negate a series of positives. That is, $(+)(+)(+)(+)(+)(+)(-) = (-)$. Looking at this from a production point of view, a bottleneck operation will determine the throughput of a overall production system. From a group operation point of view, the last passenger on a complimentary shuttle bus determines the departure time of the bus. What all these examples mean in the context of project scheduling is that our focus should be on the critical activities in the project network diagram. For the purpose of managing time breakdown of tasks that make up a project, you need to recognize the following constraints:

- Policy-based restrictions on activity time splitting
- Physical or technical limitations on activity time splitting
- Project environment limitations on activity time splitting

Each constraint type impacts the project differently. For project scheduling purposes, the critical chain is used to generate several alterations to the traditional network of project activities. All individual activity slacks or buffers become the overall project buffer. Each team member, responsible for his or her component of the activity network, creates a duration estimate free from any padding. The typical approach is to estimate time based on a 50% probability of success. All activities on the critical chain (path) and feeder chains (non-critical chains in the network) then are linked with minimal time padding. The project buffer now is aggregated and some proportion of the saved time is added to the project. Even adding 50% of the saved time significantly reduces the overall project schedule while requiring team members to be concerned less with activity padding and more with task completion. Even if the project team members miss their delivery date 50% of the time, the overall effect on the project's duration is minimized because of the downstream aggregated buffer.

If the concept of time breakdown structure presented in this chapter is followed, you can use the critical chain approach for tasks that are not on the critical chain. Accordingly, all feeder path activities are reduced by the same order of magnitude and a feeder buffer is constructed for the overall non-critical chain of activities. It should be noted that critical chain distinguishes between its use of buffer and the traditional project network use of project slack. Project slack is a function of the overall completed activity network. In other words, a slack is an outcome of the task dependencies, whereas critical chain buffer is used for planning and it is based on a logical redesign of each activity. The lesson conveyed in this chapter is that instead of lumping activity times into a big block, the elements that make up the block should be recognized and identified for the purpose of a better management practice along the line of using the 8 by 3 paradigm.

CHAPTER 5

COST BREAKDOWN STRUCTURE

"You must know where your cost is buried."
– Adedeji Badiru, Author

Just as in the corporate environment, cost tracking is an important aspect of personal time management. Understanding how cost breakdowns affect an overall goal makes it easier to manage how personal time is allocated. This is directly relevant for implementing the 8 by 3 paradigm. Money, as an object of cost, is a concern for everyone. Thus, understanding some basic concepts of cost can lead to saving money and, consequently, time. The decision of rent, lease, or buy, which more and more consumers face frequently, has its basis in an understanding of cost breakdowns. Likewise, the decision of whether to do it yourself (DIY) or hire an expert is faced by homeowners again and again. These decision scenarios have direct time management implications. For example, if you choose to use DIY to undertake a repair in your home, you need to consider the following:

- How much the repair man will cost?
- How long will it take the repair man?
- Will you have to provide some "hang-around-and-watch" time to monitor the repair man?
- If you choose to do it yourself, do you have the time?
- If you do commit your personal time to do the repair, how will you save how much your personal time is worth, in terms of opportunity cost of your not being at work earning a salary?

- Is the DIY time that you allocate for the repair detracting you away from other priorities?
- Do you have sufficient skills for the DIY project to avoid a costly rework?

These considerations influence the decision of how you allocate your time and cost, within the context of the 8 by 3 paradigm. The term "cost management" refers to the functions required to maintain effective monetary control of your endeavors. The currency denomination figure below offers a motivational representation of a cost breakdown structure.

Within a given scope of analysis, there may be a combination of different types of cost aspects to consider. These cost aspects include the ones explained below:

Actual cost of work performed: the cost actually incurred and recorded in accomplishing the work performed within a given period of time.

Applied Direct Cost: the amounts recognized in the time period associated with the consumption of labor, material, and other direct resources, without regard to the date of commitment or the date of payment. These amounts are charged to the work-in-process (WIP) when resources are actually consumed, material resources are withdrawn from inventory for use, or material resources are received and scheduled for use within the planning horizon.

Budgeted cost for work performed: the sum of the budgets for completed work plus the appropriate portion of the budgets for the level of effort and apportioned effort. Apportioned effort is effort that, by itself, is not readily divisible into short-span work packages but is related in direct proportion to the measured effort.

Budgeted cost for work scheduled: the sum of budgets for all work packages and planning packages scheduled to be accomplished (including work in process) plus the amount of level of effort and apportioned effort scheduled to be accomplished within a given period of time.

Direct cost: cost that is directly associated with actual operations of a project. Typical sources of direct costs are direct material costs and direct labor costs. Direct costs are those that can be reasonably measured and allocated to a specific component of a project.

Economies of Scale: a reduction of the relative weight of the fixed cost in the total cost by increasing output quantity. This helps to reduce the final unit cost of an undertaking. Economies of scale are often simply referred to as the savings due to mass production.

Estimated cost at completion: the actual direct costs, plus indirect costs that can be allocated to the project, plus estimated costs (direct and indirect) for the authorized work remaining.

First cost: the total initial investment required to initiate a project or the total initial cost of the equipment needed to start the project.

Fixed cost: a cost incurred irrespective of the level of operation of a project. Fixed costs do not vary in proportion to the quantity of output. Examples of costs that make up the fixed cost of a project are administrative expenses, certain types of taxes, insurance cost, depreciation cost, and debt-servicing cost. These costs usually do not vary in proportion to the quantity of output.

Incremental cost: the additional cost of changing the production output from one level to another. Incremental costs are normally variable costs.

Indirect cost: a cost that is indirectly associated with project operations. Indirect costs are those that are difficult to assign to specific components of a project. An example of an indirect cost is the cost of computer hardware and software needed to manage project operations. Indirect costs are usually calculated as a percentage of a component of direct costs. For example, the indirect costs may be computed as 10% of direct labor costs.

Life-cycle cost: the sum of all costs, recurring and nonrecurring, associated with a project during its entire life cycle. Individuals typically don't recognize the life-cycle costs of their household projects. For example, a DIY project may cost a home owner less initially upfront, but may have recurring later costs not previously anticipated or estimated by the homeowner. These costs may include cost of repair, cost of redo, or cost of calling in an expert repair man in an emergency.

Maintenance cost: a cost that occurs intermittently or periodically and is used for the purpose of keeping project equipment or resources in good operating condition.

Marginal cost: the additional cost of increasing production output by one additional unit. The marginal cost is equal to the slope of the total cost curve or line at the current operating level.

Operating cost: a recurring cost needed to keep a project in operation during its life cycle. Operating costs may consist of such items as labor cost, material cost, and energy cost.

Opportunity cost: the cost of forgoing the opportunity to invest in a venture that would have produced an economic advantage. Opportunity costs are usually incurred due to limited resources that make it impossible to take advantage of all investment opportunities. This is often defined as the cost of the best rejected opportunity. Opportunity costs can also be incurred due to a missed opportunity rather than due to an intentional rejection. In many cases, opportunity costs are hidden or implied because they typically relate to future events that cannot be accurately predicted.

Overhead cost: a cost incurred for activities performed in support of the operations of a project. The activities that generate overhead costs support the project efforts rather than contribute directly to the project goal. The handling of overhead costs varies widely from company to company. Typical overhead items are electric power cost, insurance premiums, cost of security, and inventory carrying cost.

Standard cost: a cost that represents the normal or expected cost of a unit of the output of an operation. Standard costs are established in advance. They are developed as a composite of several elemental costs, such as direct labor cost per unit, material cost per unit, and allowable overhead charge per unit.

Sunk cost: This is a cost that occurred in the past and cannot be recovered under the present scenario. Sunk costs should have no bearing on the prevailing economic analysis and project decisions. Ignoring sunk costs is always a difficult task for individuals. For example, if $50,000 was spent four years ago to buy a piece of equipment, a decision on whether or not to replace the equipment now should not consider that initial cost. But sentiments may make it difficult to ignore so much money invested upfront. Similarly, an individual making a decision on selling a personal automobile would typically try to relate the asking price to what was paid for the automobile when it was acquired. This is untenable under the concept of sunk costs.

Total cost: the sum of all the variable and fixed costs associated with a project.

Variable cost: a cost that varies in direct proportion to the level of operation or quantity of output. For example, the costs of material and labor required to make an item are categorized as variable costs since they vary with changes in the level of output.

Cost estimation and budgeting help establish a strategy for allocating resources to endeavors. There are three major categories of cost estimation for budgeting based on the desired level of accuracy:

1. Order-of-magnitude estimates
2. Preliminary cost estimates
3. Detailed cost estimates

Order-of-magnitude cost estimates are usually gross estimates based on the experience and judgment of the estimator. They are sometimes called "ballpark" figures. These estimates are typically made without a formal evaluation of the details involved in the project. Order-of-magnitude estimates can range, in terms of accuracy, from -50% to +50% of the actual cost. Preliminary cost estimates are also gross estimates, but with a higher level of accuracy. In developing preliminary cost estimates, more attention is paid to some selected details of the project. An example of a preliminary cost estimate is the estimation of expected labor cost. Preliminary estimates are useful for evaluating project alternatives before final commitments are made. The level of accuracy associated with preliminary estimates can ranges from -20% to +20% of the actual cost. Detailed cost estimates are developed after careful consideration is given to all the major details of a project. Considerable time is typically needed to obtain detailed cost estimates. Because of the amount of time and effort needed to develop detailed cost estimates, the estimates are usually developed after there is a firm commitment that the project will happen. Detailed cost estimates are also important for evaluating actual cost performance during the project. The level of accuracy associated with detailed estimates normally range from -5% to +5% of the actual cost. There are two basic approaches to generating cost estimates. The first one is a variant approach, in which cost estimates are based on variations of previous cost records. The other approach is the generative cost estimation, in which cost estimates are developed from scratch without taking previous cost records into consideration.

OPTIMISTIC AND PESSIMISTIC COST ESTIMATES

Cost estimates can fall in one of the following three categories:

- Optimistic cost estimate
- Most likely cost estimate
- Pessimistic cost estimate

In a corporate process, the most likely estimated is guessed to be four times as likely to occur as either the optimistic or pessimistic times. Thus, the average or expected cost is calculated as the optimistic estimate plus four times the most likely estimate plus the pessimistic estimate, all divided by six. This average calculation provides a reasonable guidance of what an endeavor can cost. Having a good estimate for cost expectations can guide the allocation of time to the tasks that have to be done within each block of 8-by-3 paradigm.

DISTRIBUTION OF TIME AND COST

We will get a better handle on cost and time management if we can determine where costs are allocated. Where cost goes, time follows and vice versa. A Pareto Chart is a simple tool for analyzing cost and time distribution. The chart can help to view the causes of a problem in the order of severity from the largest to the smallest. The Pareto principle of 80-20 distribution rule is commonly expressed in the operational statements below:

> 20% of your activities consume 80% of your cost.
> 20% of your project takes up 80% of your project time.

This states that, for many items, about 80% of the value comes from 20% of the items. This is often stated as the rule of the "vital few" and the "trivial many." For the purpose of implementing the 8 by 3 paradigm, activities may be put into Pareto categories for a more efficient control of the time and cost associated with the activities. The Pareto distribution can be extended to the ABC analysis, in which items are put into A, B, and C categories having different levels of significance. The categories are handled and controlled differently based on their differing levels of significance. In the ABC distribution, the following applies:

- The 'A' items are very important. These require the greatest attention.
- The B' items are important. These require moderate attention.
- The 'C' items are marginally important. These require less attention.

There are no fixed cut-off points for each category. Different percentage levels can be applied based on the prevailing circumstance and the needs of the user. Some examples are presented below:

'A' items make up 20% of the project, but accounts for 70% of the total project time.

'B' items make up 30% of the project, accounts for 25% of the total project time.

'C' items make up 50% of the project, but accounts for 5% of the total project time.

The figure below illustrates the Pareto distribution and the ABC classification.

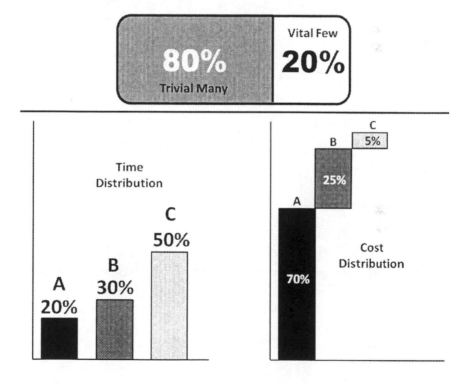

COST AND TIME MONITORING

"Where time goes, cost follows."
– Adedeji Badiru, Author

Time and cost are often linked. Like they say, "time is money." If we can manage our time effectively, we can have a better control of our cost. As a project progresses, costs can be monitored and evaluated to identify areas of unacceptable cost performance. The figure below shows a hypothetical conceptual plot of cost versus time for the planned cost and the actual cost. The plot permits a quick identification of when cost overruns occur in a project life cycle. In accordance with the 8 by 3 paradigm of time management, monitoring cost provides an avenue for a more effective management of time.

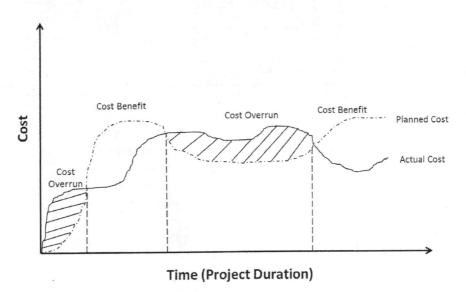

CHAPTER 6

MEASURES OF TIME EFFICIENCY

"The grass is always greener where you most need it to be dead."
– Adedeji Badiru, Author

Performance management and output assessment are essential for determining efficiency and effectiveness of actions. As the opening quote above suggests, you cannot wish away problems. Problems must be identified, confronted, and controlled. Since the focus of the 8 by 3 paradigm is on using time more efficiently, it is important to understand what efficiency implies and how to assess it so that control actions can be taken if necessary. Performance can be defined in terms of several specific metrics along different axes as illustrated in the figure below. Examples are efficiency, effectiveness, and productivity, which usually go hand-in-hand. The common business techniques for improving efficiency, effectiveness, and productivity are quite amenable for personal adaptation. Efficiency refers to the extent to which a resource (time, money, effort, etc.) is properly utilized to achieve an expected outcome. The goal, thus, is to minimize resource expenditure, reduce waste, eliminate unnecessary effort, and maximize output. The ideal (i.e., the perfect case) is to have 100% efficiency. This is rarely possible in practice. Usually expressed as a percentage, efficiency is computed as the ratio of output over input. That is, efficiency is output divided by input or result divided by effort. This ratio is also adapted for measuring productivity. For the purpose of improving personal efficiency, the 8 by 3 paradigm defines operational efficiency as follows: Operational efficiency involves a scenario, whereby all individuals coordinate their respective activities, considering all the relevant factors, such that the overall personal goals can be achieved with symbiotic input-process-output relationships with the minimum expenditure of resources yielding maximum possible outputs.

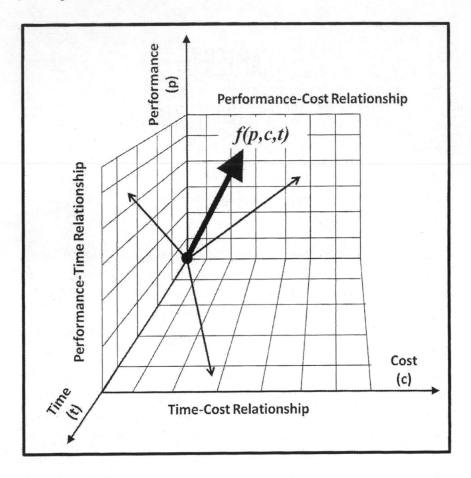

Effectiveness is a nebulous evaluative term that is difficult to quantify. It is primarily concerned with achieving the specific objectives, which constitute the broad goals of an organization. To model effectiveness quantitatively, we can consider the fact that an "objective" is essentially an "output" related to the numerator of the efficiency equation. Thus, we can assess the extent to which the various objectives of an individual are met with respect to the available resources. Although efficiency and effectiveness often go hand-in-hand, they are, indeed, different and distinct. For example, one can forego efficiency for the sake of getting a particular objective accomplished.

Consider the statement "if we can get it done, money is no object." Emergency cases often operate this way. If, for instance, our goal is to go from point A to point B to accomplish an objective; and we do achieve the objective, no matter what it takes, then we are effective. We may not be efficient based on the amount of resources expended to achieve the objective. For the purpose of this book, a cost-based measure of effectiveness is defined as the level of satisfaction divided by the cost of achieving that satisfaction. The measure of effectiveness is within the interval of zero to one, level of satisfaction of the objective is rated on a scale of zero to one, and the cost of achieving the objective is expressed on a pertinent cost basis, such as money, time, measurable resources, and so on.

If an objective is fully achieved, its satisfaction rating will be one. If not achieved at all, it will be zero. Thus, having the cost in the denominator gives a measure of achieving the objective per unit cost. If the effectiveness measures of achieving several objectives are to be compared, then the denominator (i.e., cost) will need to be normalized to a uniform scale. The overall personal effectiveness can be computed as a summation of the normalized effectiveness of each of the various objectives. Because of the potential for the effectiveness measure to be very small based on the magnitude of the cost denominator, it is essential to scale the above measure to a scale of 0 to 100. Thus, the highest comparative effectiveness per unit cost will be 100 while the lowest will be 0. The above measure of effectiveness makes most sense when comparing alternatives for achieving a specific objective. If the effectiveness of achieving an objective in absolute (non-comparative) terms is desired, it would be necessary to determine the range of costs, minimum to maximum, applicable for achieving the objective. Then, we can assess how well we satisfy the objective with the expenditure of the maximum cost versus the expenditure of the minimum cost. By analogy, "killing two birds with one stone" is efficient. By comparison, the question of effectiveness is whether we kill a bird with one stone or kill the same bird with two stones, if the primary goal is to kill the bird nonetheless. In personal management terms, pursuits that are implemented with parallel redundancy can be effective, but not necessarily efficient. In other words, a backup arrangement or a contingency plan may not be efficient, but could be effective.

In such cases, the goal is to be effective (get the job done) rather than to be efficient.

PRODUCTIVITY ASSESSMENT

Productivity is a measure of accomplishment (throughput) per unit time. The traditional application of productivity computation is in the production environment with countable or measurable units of output in repetitive operations. Manufacturing is a perfect scenario for productivity computations. In the home environment, for example, a productivity measure may pertain to how many meal servings can be produced within one hour. Typically, productivity is represented as output quantify divided by the input quantity. Applying the utilization percentage to this ratio modifies the ratio to provide an actual productivity yield. For the personal environment, which is a non-manufacturing setting, productivity analysis is still of interest. The home environment is composed, primarily, of family members, relatives, and friends, whose productivity must be measured in alternate terms, perhaps through personal work rate analysis. A simple measure of group or team output is represented as productivity multiplied by the level of effort. Productivity is expressed as a yield per person-time while effort is represented as duration times the number of people. Efficiency, effectiveness, and productivity are not simply a matter of resource availability. A person or an organization with ample resources can still be inefficient, ineffective, and unproductive. Thus, personal impediments and obstacles, apart from resource availability, should be identified and mitigated. This can be done with respect to each person's hierarchy of needs. Examples of self-inflicted impediments are ambiguous goals, undefined objectives, and unrealistic expectations. Managing one's blocks of time using the 8 by 3 paradigm can help in resolving the problem of getting many things done efficiently and effectively.

CHAPTER 7

MANAGING TIME ROBBERS

"Time robber preemption is better than time robber correction."
– Adedeji Badiru, Author

Time robbers are non-value-adding activities that creep into our schedules. Many times, we engage time robbers deliberately and consciously, even though we may not immediately realize their adverse impacts on our overall time efficiency. Sometimes, time robbers encroach into our schedules "uninvited." The 8 by 3 paradigm can help mitigate the adverse effects of both conscious and sub-conscious time robbers. This can be accomplished through the explicit technique of activity scheduling, which allocates a time block for each activity. By explicit scheduling of activities, time robbers can be more easily identified upfront and preempted. If a time robber is allowed to encroach and entrench itself into our schedule, it may be difficult to eradicate later on. For this reason, the tenet offered by the chapter opening quote above is relevant for the implementation of the 8 by 3 paradigm of time management.

Activity sequencing is the time-phased scheduling of activities subject to precedence relationships, time constraints, and resource limitations to accomplish specific objectives. The critical path method (CPM) is a network technique that presents a visual representation of activity sequencing. CPM charts are excellent visual communication tools for conveying project scope, requirements, and lines of responsibility. A project consists of activities that are mapped against a timeline. A simple example is illustrated in the figure below. Projects usually involve one-time endeavors that may not necessarily be duplicated in identical circumstances. In some cases, it may be possible to duplicate the concepts of the whole project or a portion of it in subsequent executions of the project. Several techniques are available for planning, scheduling, and controlling projects. The available scheduling techniques and solution approaches can be categorized as follows:

- Unconstrained resources
- Critical path analysis
- Time-cost trade-off problem
- Constrained resources
- Rule-of-thump techniques
- Mathematical techniques

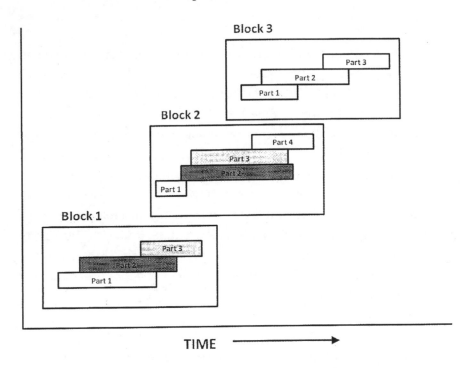

Project schedules may be complex, unpredictable, and dynamic. Complexity may be due to interdependencies of activities, multiple resource requirements, multiple concurrent events, multiple conflicting objectives, technical constraints, and schedule conflicts. Unpredictability may be due to equipment breakdowns, raw material inconsistency (delivery and quality), operator performance, worker absenteeism, and unforeseen events. Dynamism may be due to resource variability, changes in scope of work, and resource substitutions.

Predictive scheduling is a proactive scheduling approach that attempts to anticipate the potential causes of schedule problems. These problems are corrected by contingency plans. Reactive scheduling is a scheduling approach that reacts to problems that develop during project execution. The premise of the 8 by 3 paradigm is to preempt reactive scheduling of activities. If activities are scheduled to take place during their assigned blocks of time, the need for reactive and corrective reshuffling of activities will be minimized.

Network planning is sometimes referred to as activity planning. This involves the identification of the relevant activities making up a project. The required activities and their precedence relationships are determined. Precedence requirements may be determined on the basis of the following:

1. Technical limitations
2. Procedural requirements
3. Imposed constraints

Technical precedence requirements are caused by the technical relationships among activities in a project. For example, in the conventional construction of a building, walls must be erected before the roof can be installed. Procedural precedence requirements are determined by policies and procedures. Such policies and procedures are often subjective without a sound justification. Imposed precedence requirements can be classified as resource-imposed, scenario-imposed, or environment-imposed. For example, resource shortages may require that one task be scheduled before another. The current status of a project (e.g., percent completion) may determine that one activity be performed before another. The environment of a project, for example, weather changes or the effects of concurrent projects, may determine the precedence relationships of the activities in a project. Based on these precedence relationships, the activities in the project are sequenced pictorially to form a project network diagram. Time, cost, and resource requirement estimates are developed for each activity during the network planning phase. The estimates may be based on personal preference, historical records, time standards, forecasting, regression functions, or other data-based models.

Network scheduling is performed by using forward-pass and backward-pass calculations. These calculations give the earliest and latest starting and finishing times for each activity. The amount of slack associated with each activity is also determined during the calculation process. The activity path with the minimum slack in the network is used to determine the critical activities. This path also determines the duration of the project. Resource allocation, and time-cost trade-offs are other functions performed during network scheduling. The critical activities, thus determined, represent where the project should focus its attention. These high-priority activities fit the concept and procedures of the 8 by 3 paradigm of time management. Network control involves tracking the progress of a project on the basis of the network schedule and taking corrective actions when needed. An evaluation of actual performance versus expected performance determines deficiencies in the project progress. The advantages of activity sequencing for project control include the following:

- Advantages for communication
  i)   Clarification of objectives
  ii) Establishment of the specifications for project performance
  iii) Provision of a starting point for more detailed task analysis
  iv) Representation of a documentation of the project plan
  v)   Pictorial representation of the project scope

- Advantages for control
  i)   Presentation of a measure for evaluating project performance
  ii) Help in determining what corrective actions are needed
  iii) Presentation of a clear message of what is expected
  iv) Encouragement for follow up projects

- Advantages for team interaction
  - i) A mechanism for a quick introduction to the project
  - ii) Specification of functional interfaces of the project
  - iii) Facilitation of teamwork

BLOCK-BASED SEQUENCING OF ACTIVITIES

For the purpose of a practical implementation of the 8 by 3 paradigm, the blocks really don't have to be equal in duration or finitely bounded. Depending on each person's needs, the block may be sequenced as shown in the figure below, with each block filled with activity scheduling fitting the user's specific needs. For example, for those working permanent night duties, such as doctors, nurses, and security personnel, it may be necessary to customize the blocks to their specific and unique work situations.

Signatures create more bottlenecks in the corporate world than anything else of the same time magnitude. The act of signing a document, itself, does not consume much time, but the wait time to obtain a high-level signature can be problematic in the overall activity scheduling process. Also, an erroneous preparation of a document to be signed can be a source of a lengthy delay. For example re-doing and re-signing a document can consume a lot of time that is not planned or scheduled into the work process. It is essential to be prudent upfront to preempt rework and time delays.

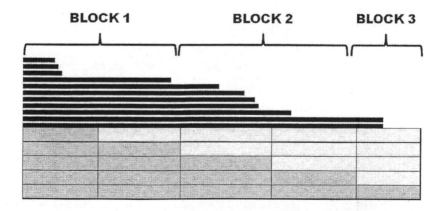

When scheduling multiple activities over several days, don't try to do too much all at the same time. Being overloaded can lead to inefficient use of time. Rather, it is expedient to attempt to accomplish at least one major task each day. Some common examples are:

- Complete income tax paperwork
- Pay bills
- Take car for service
- Exercise
- Do laundry
- Do auto registration
- Do grocery shopping
- Mow the lawn
- Reorganize file cabinet
- Send out party invitation cards

If an item is not scheduled, it may not get done. By scheduling and focusing on major activity completions one at a time, one item will not get in the way of another, thereby preserving the integrity of the 8 by 3 paradigm.

One of the nuances of my own practice of the 8 by 3 paradigm is what I do on a banquet buffet line. When the buffet line gives you one plate for the main course, one plate for dessert, and one plate for salad; and you only have two hands, what are you going to do?

1. You can juggle all three plates and run the risk of dropping one, which will cost you some clean up time.
2. You can take two plates and come back for the third later on, which will cost you some "wasteful" travel time.
3. Or you can do what I do. Merge two plates into one (e.g., dessert on the side of the salad plate); after all, they are all going to end up in the same place. This approach saves you time and minimizes your plate-dropping risk.

The moral of this practice is that every little time-saving opportunity counts. The 8 by 3 paradigm creates opportunities to save time throughout the day, thereby making it possible to get more things done within a limited period of time.

CHAPTER 8

WORK RATE AND TIME

"I like work; it fascinates me. I can sit and look at it for hours."
– Jerome K Jerome, Comedian

The chapter opening quote above begs the question: "What is the work rate of looking at work for hours?" Work rate measurement is a simple technique of measuring and assessing how quickly (or slowly) work is accomplished. When team members work concurrently at different work rates, the amount of work accomplished by each may be computed by work rate calculations. The general relationship between work, work rate and time is that work is equal to the work rate multiplied by the work duration. Work is the amount of actual output accomplished. This is expressed in appropriate units, such as miles of road completed, lines of computer codes typed, gallons of oil spill cleaned, units of widgets produced, surface area painted, or number of donuts made. Work rate per unit time is the rate at which the assigned work is accomplished. Duration is how long it times to accomplish the work. Relative cost, time, and quality measurements are essential for work rate time measurement as illustrated in the scale graphic below.

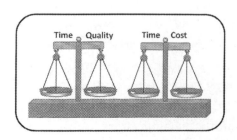

It is assumed that work rates remain constant for the duration of the work being analyzed. Work is defined as a physical measure of accomplishment with a uniform density (i.e., homogeneous). For example, one-square-footage of construction may be said to be homogeneous if one-square-footage is as complex and desirable as any other square footage. Hamburger production is homogenous if the production process is uniform and consistent, thereby making all hamburgers equally satisfying in taste, value, cost, weight, and so on. Similarly, cleaning one gallon of oil spill is as good as cleaning any other gallon of oil spill within the same work environment. The production of one unit of a product is identical to the production of any other unit of the production of any other unit of the same product. If a uniform work density can be assumed for the particular work being analyzed, then the relationship is defined as one whole unit, and the following relationship will be applicable for the case of a single person performing the work: Work rate multiplied by the work duration equals one whole unit of work.

For example, if a construction worker can build one block in 30 minutes, then his work rate is 1/30 of a block per minute. If the magnitude of the denominator of the work rate is greater than the magnitude of the work duration, then only a fraction of the required work will be performed. The information about the proportion of work completed is useful for work planning, time allotment, and productivity measurement purposes. In the case of many people performing the work simultaneously as a team, the work relationship is expanded by summation to account for the group output relative to individual outputs. The examples that follow illustrate work rate calculations.

Suppose Person 1, working alone, can complete a job in 50 hours. After Person 1 has been working on the job for 10 hours, Person 2 was assigned to help Person 1 in completing the job. Both workers, working together, finished the remaining work in 15 hours. It is desired to determine the work rate of Person 2. The amount of work to be done is 1.0 whole unit. The work rate of Person 1 is 1/50 of work per unit time. Therefore, the amount of work completed by Person 1 in the 10 days he or she worked alone is $(1/50)(10)=1/5$ of the required work. This may also be expressed in terms of percent completion. The remaining work to be done is 4/5 of the total work.

The two workers working together for 15 hours produce the following result: 15/50 +15(work rate of Person 2) = 45, which yields1/30 for the work rate of Person 2. This means that Person 2, working alone, could perform the job in 30 hours. In this example, it is assumed that both workers produce identical quality of work. If quality levels are not identical for multiple workers, then the work rates may be adjusted to account for the different quality levels or a quality factor may be introduced into the analysis. The relative costs of the different workers needed to perform the required work may be incorporated into the analysis for a cost-based assessment.

As another example, suppose the work rate of Person 1 is such that he can perform a certain task in 30 hours. It is desired to add Person 2 to the task so that the completion time of the task could be reduced. The work rate of Person 2 is such that he can perform the same task alone in 22 hours. If Person 1 has already worked 12 hours on the task before Person 2 comes in, we want to find the completion time of the task. It is assumed that Person 1 starts the task at time 0. The amount of work to be done is 1.0 whole unit (i.e., the full task). The work rate of Person 1 is 1/30 of the task per unit time and the work rate of Person 2 is 1/22 of the task per unit time. The amount of work completed by Person 1 in the 12 hours he or she worked alone is (1/30)(12)=2/5 (or 40%) of the required work. Therefore, the remaining work to be done is 2/5 (or 60%) of the full task. Now, we let T be the time for which both people work together. Then, the two people working together to complete the task means that T/30+T/22=3/5, which yields T = 7.62 hours. Consequently, the completion time of the task is 12 + 7.62 = 19.62 hours. It is assumed that both workers produce identical quality of work and that the respective work rates remain consistent. An appreciation of the respective work rates is important in fitting activities into specific time blocks within the 8 by 3 paradigm.

CHAPTER 9

5S PRINCIPLE FOR GETTING ORGANIZED

"Tomorrow belongs to those who prepare for it today"
– African Proverb

This chapter's opening quote suggests that to do well tomorrow, we must prepare the path today. This means that being organized today will pave the way for a successful execution of tasks tomorrow. Being organized is a key requirement for managing time. For the 8 by 3 paradigm to be effective for you, you must be well organized to make proper allocations of tasks across the blocks of time. In the corporate environment, there are formal tools and techniques for organizing work. Those same techniques can be adopted for personal organization. One simple, but rigorous, approach for organizing work is the Japanese technique of 5s, which stipulates workplace discipline through a series of words starting with the letter "s." When five s-words are used, we have "5s" and when six words are used, we have "6s." The words are explained below:

1. Seiri (Sort): This means to distinguish between what is needed and not needed and remove the latter. The tools and materials in the workplace are sorted out. The unwanted tools and materials are placed in the Red Tag area, which is used for identifying, tagging, removing, and disposing of items that are not needed in the work area. It applied to the kitchen area in a home, it will mean removing from the kitchen all items not immediately needed in a typical day in the kitchen.

2. Seiton (Stabilize): This means to enforce a place for everything and everything in its place. The workplace is organized by labeling. The machines and tools are labeled with their names and all the sufficient data required. A sketch with exact scale of the work floor is drawn with grids. This helps in achieving a better flow of work and an easy access to all tools and machines.

3. Seison (Shine): This means to clean up the workplace and look for ways to keep it clean. Periodic cleaning and maintenance of the workplace and machines are done. The wastes are placed in a separate area. The recyclable and other wastes are separately placed in separate containers. This makes it easy to know where every component is placed. The clean look of the workplace helps in a better organization and increases the flow of work.

4. Seiketsu (Standardize): This means to maintain and monitor adherence to the first three s's. This process helps to standardize work. The work of each person is clearly defined. The suitable person is chosen for a particular work. People in the workplace should know who is responsible for what. The scheduling is standardized. Time is maintained for every work that is to be done. A set of rules is created to maintain the first 3s's. This helps in improving efficiency of the workplace.

5. Shitsuke (Sustain): This means to follow the rules to keep the workplace 5s-compliant to "maintain the gain." Once the previous 4s's are implemented some rules are developed for sustaining the other s's.

6. Safety: This refers to eliminating hazards in the work environment. The sixth "s" is added so that focus could be directed at safety within all improvement efforts. This is particularly essential in high-risk and accident-prone environments. This sixth extension is often debated as a separate entity because safety should be implicit in everything we do. Besides, the Japanese word for Safety is "Anzen," which does not follow the "s" rhythm. Going further out on a limb,

some practitioners even include additional levels of "s." So, we could have 8s with the addition of Security and Satisfaction.

7. Security: This could involve job security, personal security, mitigation of risk, capital security, intellectual security, property security, information security, asset security, equity security, product brand security, and so on.

8. Satisfaction: This could include personal satisfaction, employee satisfaction, morale, job satisfaction, sense of belonging, and so on.

If 5s is practiced with the seriousness of a corporate entity, a better management of time can be achieved. There is a lot of waste in our normal personal day-to-day activities. These wastes consume time in terms of tracking, storing, and maintaining. A waste is anything other than the minimum amount of equipment, materials, raw materials, parts, and storage space, which are definitely essential in adding value to work in progress. For example, in a kitchen, maintaining two sets of pots in the immediate vicinity of the stove constitutes a waste, which ultimately translates to time inefficiency.

In a corporate setting, the eight deadly wastes are identified as over production, product defects, inventory, excess process, transportation, excess motion, waiting, and under-utilizing resources (e.g., human resources). The same waste assessment can be done for the home environment, thereby identifying wasted efforts that lead to inefficient use of time. In summary, to save time, do the following:

- Things that are frequently used should be placed closer to the work bench.
- Things that are occasionally used should be located in the distant vicinity of the work site.
- Things that are rarely used should be placed in storage and out of the way.

The practice of the 5s technique complements the time blocking approach of the 8 by 3 paradigm.

CHAPTER 10

TIPS FOR 8 BY 3 TIME MANAGEMENT

"A stitch in time saves nine."
– An English Proverb

This chapter's opening quote conveys that a timely effort will preempt more later on, which is the premise of the 8 by3 paradigm. Conservation of time is the best way to save time. The tips below are offered as a guide to readers. They can be expanded to fit each person's needs and specific situations. The premise of each tip is that time can be saved by adopting time-conscious strategies at home, work, and leisure. The simple fact is that things that are done or not done have time implications somewhere down the line. If these time robbers can be preempted or averted in advance, we can avoid time-consuming corrections, reactions, or modifications later on. Issues that appear to be non-time-involved up front always turn out to have underlying time implications when viewed in the context of full ramifications. In other words, everything has a time basis in the final analysis. Below are my own original tips that I offer to the potential adopters of the 8 by 3 paradigm:

- Accept the existence of differences in others; it saves you time in dealing with them.
- Acquire new skills so that you can succeed in new environments; this costs less time.
- Anticipate obstacles; it takes less time to preempt than to fight and defeat.

- Anticipate problems and preempt them; time, thus saved, can be used for other purposes.
- Apologize promptly when needed; this saves time later on.
- Ask questions, not to criticize, but to learn more about the problem scenario.
- Assess your own talents and interests and leverage them to craft your goals and objectives.
- At work, home, or in the public, respect yourself so that others may respect you.
- At work, home, or play, follow through on commitments to create a reputation of reliability.
- Avoid loathsome disposition; it reflects back onto yourself.
- Avoid personal vendetta; it only chews up your time.
- Avoid punitive reactions; it costs time to be vengeful.
- Avoid retaliation just for the sake of getting even; there is no value in vengeance.
- Avoid silo-typical approach to your work and capability; getting help from others saves time.
- Avoid pessimism; it only sees the cloudy part of the day.
- Balance the need for additional information with the expediency of moving forward to action.
- Be a dependable steward of organizational resources; saving resources saves time.
- Be a pleasure to work with; it will take you less time to seek collaboration.
- Be approachable; intimidation will cost you more time when trying to seal a deal.
- Be consistent in your actions and utterances; dilly-dallying costs time.
- Be fair and consistent; fairness cost less time.
- Be happy with yourself, knowing that you have managed your time effectively.
- Be honest and trustworthy; this will avoid you having to spend time defending yourself.
- Be open and receptive to others' ideas; it costs less time to commend than to fight the ideas.

- Be open to new ideas; you may learn time-saving tricks.
- Be optimistic while being cognizant of potential pitfalls.
- Be reliable and dependable; it will save you time in your interactions with others.
- Be SMART with your engagements (Specific, Measurable, Achievable, Realistic, Timed).
- Be tolerant of the views of others; there is a gem in everyone.
- Be willing to learn from your subordinates; you don't have all the answers.
- Challenge yourself and thrive as you overcome the pain of tribulations.
- Communicate to inspire others; they may reciprocate with time-saving kindness.
- Compliment often; it doesn't cost time or money.
- Conserve time; it is the basis for all endeavors.
- Coordinate responsibilities to facilitate expeditious completion of projects.
- Delegate as needed so that you can direct your time toward more critical needs.
- Demonstrate a positive attitude regardless of the prevailing challenges.
- Demonstrate professionalism in all you do.
- Develop a passion for self-advancement; time efficiency in around the corner.
- Develop a vision and share it with others; they will be there to assist you.
- Develop an inclusive embrace for co-workers; they will accept you and save you time.
- Develop and sustain a "can-do" attitude to all challenges; giving up early is the door of failure.
- Discpline yourself when you have erred; this avoids having someone else do it.
- Do actual work to pass the time; do not whine away the time with complaints about work.
- Do it and forget it, so that you may move on to spending your time on other things.

- Do the right thing when no one is watching; personal gratification is as good as public accolades.
- Do the right thing the first time, so that you won't have to spend time doing it over again.
- Do things fast; timely execution of tasks creates more time for the next achievement.
- Do now, what you need to do. There is never a better time to do it.
- Do what you must before being forced to do it; being proactive saves time.
- Don't be a hard-baller; give-and-take takes the day in the long run.
- Don't be a procrastinator extraordinaire. Do it now, if you are going to do it at all.
- Don't blame others for your own failings; acceptance is the first order of getting better.
- Don't despair when a failure occurs; there is always a way to make amendments.
- Don't dilly-dally on simple decisions that have no business being delayed.
- Don't do Winter projects in the Summer and don't do Summer project in the Winter; it will cost you more time to flip-flop projects.
- Don't let minor problems fester into bigger problems, which will cost you more time.
- Don't multitask incompatible tasks; decoupling overlapped tasks costs more time.
- Don't put off what can be done and dismissed now.
- Don't try to do too much; being overstretched will erode your productivity.
- Don't try to do too many things at once; it leads to costly cut-corner temptations.
- Don't while away your time by engaging in destructive whining.
- Embrace the notion that preemption is better than correction.
- Embrace, promote, and leverage change; it is good for keeping things lively.
- Evaluate alternatives and new perspectives; new discoveries may be found.

- Exhibit empathy and compassion for others; you may need same from them some day.
- Exhibit respect for others; it will save you time when they reciprocate.
- Focus on a positive outcome even if the path is paved with difficulties.
- Focus on the end result; it provides "light-at-the-end-of-the-tunnel" motivation.
- Have respect for time; it is the basis for all your accomplishments.
- Identify and focus on the most significant priorities.
- Imagine possibilities and opportunities; that is where success resides.
- In the work place, whether you are the boss or the underling, contribute to the work environment in a way that makes everyone feel valued.
- Interact with others positively; remember the Biblical exhortation of "Do unto others as you would have others do unto you."
- Keep priorities few and manageable; over-ambition paves the way for disappointment.
- Keep things simple; it takes less time to do simple things.
- Know that life-long learning leads to a longer life.
- Know that proactive ethical standards avoid time-consuming corrective actions later on.
- Know that a shared vision is better than a solo vision.
- Know that what is worth doing at all is worth doing now (or soon).
- Lead by example always; be prepared to follow as needed.
- Leverage your personal knowledge and experience in your decision-making processes.
- Link the current situation to guide future expectations and time management.
- Listen and learn; you cannot learn while talking.
- Listen well the first time; having to be told again will cost you time.
- Live by optimism; it sees only the rays of sunshine of the day and hope for the future.

- Maintain a vibrant perspective; stagnancy gets no one no where.
- Maintain upright personal behavior to enhance performance.
- Manage your emotions as tightly as you manage your time.
- Minimize travel in bad weather; getting stuck will cost you time.
- Monitor, track, and re-evaluate the execution of your plans.
- Preserve time; it is the foundation for success.
- Put organizational needs above personal gains; a successful organization is your success.
- Put others at ease; you gain more by not scaring people off.
- Put principles above personality in work relationships; being principled saves time.
- Recognize and acknowledge the contributions of others.
- Recognize internal and external factors influencing your actions.
- Recognize problems before they take root.
- Recognize that everything is time-sensitive; putting something off costs more time later.
- Recognize that foresight enhances hindsight.
- Recognize that later is not necessarily better when executing tasks.
- Recognize that no situation is permanent (except death); "up" can become "down" and vice versa.
- Recognize that the "do-nothing" alternative is always an option; it may be less time costly.
- Respond with calmness and composure; an agitated reaction clouds good judgment.
- Retire to bed early; most bad things happen at night.
- Reward yourself when you have earned it; this provides a lasting motivation.
- Schedule your daytime well; so that you won't have to roam the night.
- Seek cooperation explicitly from those you work with.
- Seek new innovative ways to improve things.
- Solve problems from an integrative perspective; integration saves time.
- Stand behind your decisions; a firm stand costs less time.
- Stand by those who stand by you.

- Stick to your budget; budget consistency requires less time to manage.
- Strive to do the right thing always; the right thing is right for saving time.
- Support others so that they may support you.
- Swallow your pride when necessary; it will cost you less time to make amendments.
- Take responsibility for your own actions.
- Task yourself to be a positive role model always.
- Think of consequences before embarking on time costly actions.
- Note that time management requires the same level of dedication and seriousness that we apply to our money management.
- Train others to have the skills to pick up slacks that may help lessen your own load.
- Train others to help you with your own objectives.
- Use available data to develop accurate and relevant decision analysis.
- Use mistakes as learning opportunities to leverage in moving on to the next accomplishment.
- Use personal leadership to exercise self-management and time control.
- Use past experience to direct future goal setting.
- Use cold and wet days for indoor chores and use warm and dry days for outdoor chores.
- View the world as a system of inter-connected needs and requirements.
- Walk when you can; your health is worth the walk.
- Why not do now, what you are going to do eventually?

PROBLEM PREEMPTION TIPS TO SAVE TIME

<u>On the road</u>:

- Think safety first and foremost.
- Note that haste makes waste in the end.

- Anticipate the stupid acts of other drivers.
- Be mindful that if it is stupidly possible, some driver will do it.
- Be defensive-minded around other drivers.
- Act as if you are the other drivers' keeper.
- Be a responsible shared-road user.
- Avoid reckless driving so that road problems will avoid you.
- Know that your destination is not running away; why do you have to chase it?
- Know that easy does it; hard-nosed driving will lead to a hard break.
- Don't drink and drive; the 8 by 3 model allocates time for each task.
- Don't text and drive; communication never expires, it will still be there.
- Predetermine a safe route to travel; avoid last-minute brash moves.
- Eat before you drive; avoid hunger-induced food fidgeting on the steering wheel.
- Recognize that foot and bike traffic is a part of the overall traffic system.
- If you see a car in traffic with banged up bumper, take note and avoid the car. The driver may have a record of involvement in traffic mishaps and may not care about tangling with your vehicle. Remember the broken window syndrome.

At home:

- Put tools where they belong so that time is saved in retrieving them later.
- Maintain good housekeeping; it makes it easier and faster to sort things out.
- Organize assets; this helps to find things when needed, thus saving time.
- Save leftovers for later use; this saves time from preparing fresh dishes too often.

- Clean as you go; accumulated dirt takes more time to clean at once.
- Don't lounge around the basement all day on a good-weather day. Get out and use the bright daylight to clean your garage, clean roof gutters, or mow the lawn.
- Do at night, what you don't need daylight to do.
- Do at daylight, what you need outside daylight to do.
- Keep yourself healthy. It is through good health that you can spend time on your tasks.
- Avoid time-robbing unhealthy habits:
- Don't smoke.
- Don't drink excessively.
- Don't drink and drive. It will eventually rob you of your time.
- Don't sacrifice your sleep. Adequate sleep rejuvenates your body, soul, and mind.
- Don't fail to get inoculations. Preventive medicine will save you from sick time.
- Don't overindulge in bad diets. Healthy eating keeps you healthy and time-efficient.
- Don't search for love in the wrong places. Time is wasted on wrong endeavors.
- Practice good personal habits:
- Eat well.
- Love well. This is the tonic for body and mind.
- Visit your doctor regularly. This helps to keep you well and time-efficient.
- Have a plan and execute your plan.
- Socialize without going overboard.

Tips for Student Application of the 8 by 3 Model:

- Sleep well; it reinvigorates the brain so that it requires less time to learn.
- Pay attention in class the first time; there will not be enough time to do it later.
- Manage your time upfront; time is irrecoverable once it is lost.

- Don't go to class late; it will cost you more time to catch up with class later on.
- Don't text, talk, or doodle in class; what you miss in class will cost more time to learn.
- Don't turn in homework late; it costs less time to do it on time and forget it.
- Study incrementally rather than in overextended blocks of time. Smaller chunks of knowledge stick better and longer.
- Allocate a bounded and limited time for friends; they can occupy your time needlessly.
- Avoid frivolous pursuits; they divert your time from meaningful activities.
- Develop and maintain good work ethics; keeping to tasks costs less time.
- Demonstrate good personal ethics; doing the right time costs less time.
- Avoid instant gratification; it comes back to bite your time later on.
- Develop a sustainable schedule for studying; a consistent study pattern requires less time.
- Recognize that education is power; invest your time in getting it at the earliest opportunity.
- Commit the quote below to your heart:

> "Education is the most powerful weapon which
> you can use to change the world."
> – Nelson Mandela

Get actively involved in learning opportunities. Direct involvement seals the deal of learning. Adopt the philosophy below:

> "Tell me and I forget;
> Show me and I remember;
> Involve me and I understand."
> – Confucius, Chinese Philosopher

PERSPECTIVES ON THE MODEL

As with any new approach, acceptance and embrace are keys to the success of the approach. The 8 by 3 paradigm is new and different from conventional approaches to managing time. A fair assessment of the strengths and weaknesses of any approach can help users make a better decision on how to embrace and utilize the new approach. The table below presents the pros and cons of the 8 by 3 model. An implementation of the new paradigm may at first appear to be difficult and overly structured. Indeed, it can be hard to be structured in these days of a rushed society and crowded lifestyles. But, as Author Thomas Carlyle reminds us, "Every noble work is at first impossible." So, give it a try and you'll be amazed how well this new paradigm can aid your time management.

PROS of 8by3 Paradigm	CONS of 8by3 Paradigm
Provides a structured guidance	May be too rigid
Provides motivation for task execution	Subject to time block violations
Provides clarity of responsibilities	Requires self-discipline (this may be good)
Easy to remember	Demarcation lines are not definite
Builds family accountability	May be painful to practice
Provides motivational guidance	Requires time to adopt
Serves as an inspiration for time management	New and unfamiliar

APPENDIX:

USEFUL TIME-RELATED CONVERSION FACTORS

A. TEMPERATURE CONVERSION FACTORS

Citation: The time of day affects the expected temperature.

<u>Conversion formulas</u>

Celsius to Kelvin	$K = C + 273.15$
Celsius to Fahrenheit	$F = (9/5)C + 32$
Fahrenheit to Celsius	$C = (5/9)(F - 32)$
Fahrenheit to Kelvin	$K = (5/9)(F + 459.67)$
Fahrenheit to Rankin	$R = F + 459.67$
Rankin to Kelvin	$K = (5/9)R$

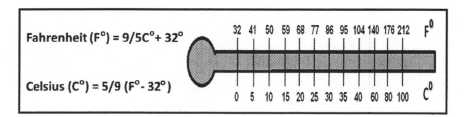

B. KITCHEN MEASUREMENT CONVERSION FACTORS

Citation: Time spent in the kitchen is affected by measurement translations

1 pinch	= 1/8 tea spoon or less
3 tea spoons	= 1 table spoon
2 table spoons	= 1/8 cup
4 table spoons	= 1/4 cup
8 table spoons	= 1/2 cup
12 table spoons	= 3/4 cup
16 table spoons	= 1 cup
5 table spoons + 1 tea spoon	= 1/3 cup
4oz	= 1/2 cup
8oz	= 1 cup
16 oz	= 1lb
1 oz	= 2 table spoons of fat or liquid
1 cup of liquid	= 1/2 pint
2 cups	= 1 pint
2 pints	= 1 quart
4 cup of liquid	= 1 quart
4 quarts	= 1 gallon
8 quarts	= 1 peck (apples, pears, etc.)
1 jigger	= 1½ fluid oz
1 jigger	= 3 table spoons

C. MICRO AND MACRO NUMBER NOTATIONS

Citation: Measurement of time requirement may range from tiny to huge, as in nanosecond and light-year time scales.

Notations and Expansions

yotta (10^{24}):	$1,000,000,000,000,000,000,000,000$
zetta (10^{21}):	$1,000,000,000,00,0\,000,000,000$
exa (10^{18}):	$1,000,000,000,000,000,000$
peta (10^{15}):	$1,000,000,000,000,000$
tera (10^{12}):	$1,000,000,000,000$
giga (10^{9}):	$1,000,000,000$
mega (10^{6}):	$1,000,000$
kilo (10^{3}):	$1,000$
hecto (10^{2}):	100
deca (10^{1}):	10
deci (10^{-1}):	0.1
centi (10^{-2}):	0.01
milli (10^{-3}):	0.001
micro (10^{-6}):	$0.000\,001$
nano (10^{-9}):	$0.000\,000\,001$
pico (10^{-12}):	$0.000\,000\,000\,001$
femto (10^{-15}):	$0.000\,000\,000\,000\,001$
atto (10^{-18}):	$0.000\,000\,000\,000\,000\,001$
zepto (10^{-21}):	$0.000\,000\,000\,000\,000\,000\,001$
yocto (10^{-24}):	$0.000\,000\,000\,000\,000\,000\,000\,001$
stringo (10^{-35}):	$0.000\,000\,000\,000\,000\,000\,000\,000\,000\,000\,01$

D. DECIMAL CONVERSION

Citation: Fraction of time implies time sensitivity, as in split-second

1/16 = 0.0625
1/8 = .125
3/16 = .1875
1/4 = .25
5/16 = .3125
3/8 = .375
7/16 = .4375
½ = .5
9/16 = .5625
5/8 = .625
11/16 = .6875
3/4 = .75
13/16 =.8125
7/8 = .875
15/16 = .9375
1 = 1.0

E. DISTANCE MEASUREMENT

Citation: Coverage of distance takes time, as in miles per hour

English system
1 foot (ft) = 12 inches (in)
1 yard (yd) = 3 feet
1 mile (mi) = 1,760 yards
1 sq. foot = 144 sq. inches
1 sq. yard = 9 sq. feet
1 acre = 4,840 sq. yards = 43,560 sq. feet
1 sq. mile = 640 acres

Metric system
mm = Millimeter (.001m)
cm = Centimeter (.01m)
dm = Decimeter (.1m)
m = Meter (1m)
dam = Decameter (10m)
hm = Hectometer (100m)
km = Kilometer (1,000m)

F. DISTANCE CONVERSION

Citation: The passage of time assures the coverage of distance

feet = 0.30480 meters = 12 inches
inches = 25.40 millimeters = 0.02540 meters = 0.08333 feet
kilometers = 3,280.8 feet = 0.6214 miles = 1,094 yards
meters = 39.370 inches = 3.2808 feet = 1.094 yards
miles = 5,280 feet = 1.6093 kilometers = 0.8694 nautical miles
millimeters = 0.03937 inches
nautical miles = 6,076 feet = 1.852 kilometers
yards = 0.9144 meters = 3 feet = 36 inches

G. VELOCITY CONVERSION FACTORS

Citation: Velocity is Distance over Time

feet/minute = 5.080 mm/second
feet/second = 0.3048 meters/second
inches/second = 0.0254 meters/second
km/hour = 0.6214 miles/hour
meters/second = 3.2808 feet/second = 2.237 miles/hour
miles/hour = 88.0 feet/minute = 0.44704 meters/second = 1.6093 km/hour
= 0.8684 knots
knot = 1.151 miles/hour

H. VOLUME CONVERSION FACTORS

Citation: Flow rate per unit time is related to volume, as in flood rate

acre-foot = 1,233.5 cubic meters
cubic cm = 0.06102 cubic inches
cubic feet = 1,728 cu. inches = 7.480 gallons (US) = 0.02832 cu. meters =
0.03704 cu. Yards
liter = 1.057 = liquid quarts = 0.908 dry quarts = 61.024 cubic inches
gallons (US) = 231 cu. in = 3.7854 liters = 4 quarts = 0.833 British gallons
= 128 US fluid oz.
quarts(US) = 0.9463 liters

I. TIME-RELATED ENERGY CONVERSION

Citation: Energy consumption is a function of time, as in watts per second

BTU = 1,055.9 joules = 0.2520 kg-calories
Watt-hour = 3,600 joules = 3.409 BTU
HP (electric) = 746 watts
BTU/second = 1,055.9 watts
Watt-second = 1 joule

J. TIME-BASED CONSTANTS

Citation: The passage of time is constant

Speed of light = $2.997,925 \times 10^{10}$ cm/sec = 983.6×10^{10} ft/sec = 186,284 miles/sec
Velocity of sound = 340.3 meters/sec = 1116 ft/sec
Gravity (acceleration) = 9.80665 m/sec square = 32.174 ft/sec square
386.089 inches/sec square